Sophia
and
Praxis

The International Seminar for Philosophy and Political Theory gratefully acknowledges the support for its program provided by the Kemper Educational and Charitable Fund, the Earhart Foundation, and the Social Sciences and Humanities Research Council of Canada.

This book was made possible by matching subvention grants from the Kemper Educational and Charitable Fund and the University of Saskatchewan.

Sophia
and
Praxis

The Boundaries of Politics

Edited by J. M. Porter

CHATHAM HOUSE PUBLISHERS, INC.
Chatham, New Jersey

Sophia and Praxis: The Boundaries of Politics

CHATHAM HOUSE PUBLISHERS, INC.
Post Office Box One
Chatham, New Jersey 07928

PUBLISHER: Edward Artinian
DESIGNER: Quentin Fiore
COMPOSITION: Chatham Composer
PRINTING AND BINDING: Hamilton Printing Company

LIBRARY OF CONGRESS CATALOGING IN PUBLICATION DATA
Main entry under title:

Sophia and praxis.

  Papers from a conference sponsored by the Internation-
al Seminar for Philosophy and Political Theory.
  Includes bibliographical references.
  1. Political science—Congresses. I. Porter,
J.M. (Jene M.), 1937-   . II. International
Seminar for Philosophy and Political Theory.
JA35   1984   320   84-12154
ISBN 0-934540-19-5

Manufactured in the United States of America
10   9   8   7   6   5   4   3   2   1

Preface

Founded in 1979, the International Seminar for Philosophy and Political Theory is an independent academic association. It conducts programs of common research linking philosophy to the problems of politics. Representing no particular school of thought, it seeks collaboration with theorists and scholars whose interests, in our critical contemporary situation, go beyond narrow methodological, textual, or ideological consideration to consider the larger perennial questions concerning man, society, and history. The Seminar's sole commitment is to the pursuit of truth wherever it may be found. Toward this end it is devoted to the historical and philosophical study of man's search for his humanity and its order in history and society.

The purpose of the Seminar is to promote research in two primary areas:

1. The analysis of modern thought and experience through the philosophical investigation of the underlying symbolic forms of existence and their social ramifications.

2. The development of a coherent philosophy of culture and history which can provide an empirically based, theoretically sound analysis of sociopolitical order and disorder.

With assistance from the Rockefeller and Earhart Foundations, the Seminar held its preparatory session at the Rockefeller Foundation's Bellagio Study and Conference Center at Lake Como, Italy, in March 1980. Papers were read on the theme "Modern Images of Order and Disorder," and a multiyear program of research on "Politics and Its Boundaries" was discussed and established. With assistance from the Kemper Educational and Charitable Fund, the Earhart Foundation, and the Social Sciences and Humanities Research Council of Canada, the first groundwork session was held in Montreal in May 1981. This session was devoted to the topic "*Sophia* and *Praxis*." The 1982 meeting, held in Germany, examined the topic "Rhetoric, Persuasion, and Political Action." The publication of future volumes is envisaged.

JÜRGEN GEBHARDT, Co-President
DANTE GERMINO, Co-President

Contents

Introduction
J. M. PORTER

In order to understand and resuscitate the political dimension of human existence, it is necessary to perceive the relation between *sophia* (wisdom) and *praxis* (action). The common project of these essays is to demonstrate in various ways that *sophia* and *praxis* are related in a true politics. Since politics had its origins in a specific period and cultural context, it is necessary to devote some attention to the philosophic history of the pertinent terms. But since symbols and meanings are subtly changed and even transformed through history, philosophical analysis of contemporary terms and uses is also necessary. Thus, through a blend of conceptual history and analysis, these essays present a philosophic defense of a politics conceived as a public and reasoned collective action.

Reflection on the nature of politics originated in the classical Greek experience of the polis. It is Jürgen Gebhardt's thesis that this original political experience, prior to Plato and Aristotle, contained the fundamental ingredients that would lead to Greek philosophy. The centrality of the political realm can be seen in the original "political" use of such terms as *sophia* and *theoria*. Through an examination of these and other terms, Gebhardt inquires into how politics was discovered, and how with this discovery there grew the "differentiating experiences that retrospectively would become the symbolic form of philosophy."

With a careful examination of the original texts, Gebhardt traces the emerging Hellenic self-understanding of the experience of politics. The tragedies, as one example, clearly represent the politics of the citizen and the emergence of a new perception of the forces in the human soul. With the disintegration of the polis, tragedy as a representation of man's nature and condition was replaced by philosophy. There was in the early mystic philosophers, Gebhardt contends, an incipient universalism that transcended and survived the death of the polis. The initial experience and discovery of politics had led to the philosophy of politics. Thus, *sophia* was not viewed by the Greeks as the opposite of *praxis*. *Sophia,* historically, grew out of the needs and experiences of the polis. There was no polarity between inactive, abstract, scientific, and theoretical knowledge versus active, particular, and practical application. Gebhardt's essay suggests one possible perspective for understanding politics and the relation of *sophia* and *praxis*.

Even though we live in historical continuity with the past and even though the explication of the original meanings and context enables us to distinguish more clearly modern mutations, just as Gebhardt argues, we cannot simply transplant those meanings and context on to modern soil. Yet, the integration of *sophia* and *praxis* is a precondition for a politics understood as reasoned political action, that is, a politics of principles and beliefs. It is crucial, accordingly, to examine in contemporary terms the reason-action relationship or nexus, and this is the topic of Frederick Barnard's essay. Unless one can establish that there is in some sense a causal relationship between reasons and action, the idea of political action is not conceivable. Barnard presents the case that reasons can account for human action and for its subspecies political action because reasons — not rationalizations — are constitutive of action.

Through examining the concepts of rationality and causality, Barnard shows that reasons are contained in action, and thus human actions are made intelligible as meaningful conduct and are not reducible to mechanical or natural processes. Because political action has the same anatomy as individual action, it becomes at least conceivable to view politics as a reasoned activity of which an account or explanation can be given. Just as a citing of socioeconomic or psychophysical "causes" could not make intelligible what a person does for reasons, political action cannot be reduced to such mechanical or natural origins. Joint beliefs and principles or a political ideology, Barnard argues, can disclose the meaning of a political act in the same manner that a reason can account for an individual act. Political discourse, he concludes, is actually a form of rational discourse used to rally "support by providing persuasive grounds for concerted actions." The nature of political discourse becomes the theme for the next essay.

Bertrand de Jouvenel has said that the "elementary political process is the action of mind upon mind through speech." George Graham and William Havard discuss the relation between political knowledge and action in contemporary political speech and find, in agreement with Barnard, that the relation between *sophia* and *praxis* has been radically altered with the predominance of various types of "scientistic" theories of knowledge. They demonstrate that such modern epistemological considerations as an instrumental conception of reason, the separation of object and subject, and the absolute distinction between the factual and the evaluative have rendered nugatory, in their words, the relation between *sophia* and *praxis* in the practical areas of ethics and politics. Modern political discourse and rhetoric, as a consequence, atrophy.

Rhetoric is needed for political discourse and for translating political and ethical knowledge into *praxis*. After exploring the Aristotelian connections among philosophic knowledge, deliberation, education, action, and rhetoric, Graham and Havard probe the question whether contemporary politicians can be statesmen. The possibility—illustrated by brief treatments of Franklin Roosevelt, Martin Luther King, Jr., and Ronald Reagan—is dependent, they reason, not only on the statesman's rhetoric, which must be grounded on knowledge and deliberation, but on a people who have a "developed common sense *(phronesis)*" sufficient to respond to the deliberative arguments of the statesman. In this manner, *sophia* and *praxis* can be related through the statesman's art of rhetoric, and politics becomes possible.

In modernity the *sophia-praxis* relationship has been liable to two particular derailments. One is the constant attempt to separate and oppose one to the other. In the course of unfolding the arguments for their own topics, Gebhardt, Barnard, and Graham and Havard have all noted and criticized such efforts, and they have shown some of the detrimental consequences for politics. The second is the attempt, particularly common among Marxists, to conflate *praxis* and subsume *sophia*. Thomas Flanagan's essay is devoted to the first derailment, and Athanasios Moulakis dissects the second.

For this reason, the contribution by Flanagan shifts the emphasis from the philosophic origins and nature of the relationship between *sophia* and *praxis* to a direct examination and critique of a modern and perhaps prevailing conception of that relationship. Nobel laureate Friedrich Hayek has been, arguably, the most popular and famous thinker of the contemporary period who has criticized the view that a scheme of certain knowledge (a parody of *sophia*) could be applied to social reality in order to remake and construct a new society (a parody of *praxis*). There are various schemes of this sort, but all share a common philosophic structure, which Hayek calls "constructivism." Flanagan explicates Hayek's critique of constructivism and provides some needed philosophic support by relating Hayek's position to the *sophia* and *praxis* nexus.

Constructivism can be seen in the propensity to conceive of social reality as an organization amenable to the created and imposed rules of an administration. In contrast, Hayek suggests that society is a spontaneous order with rules that have evolved and are superior to any that could be devised and imposed. Language, the common law, and the market are classic illustrations of such orders. While describing Hayek, Flanagan also amends, but he does hold that Hayek's concept of constructivism is an excellent diagnosis of the tendency in modern political ideologies to have society remade through the use of state power and according to some plan or blueprint, which is in turn based upon an hubristic claim of knowledge.

In Flanagan's helpful phrase, "politics is the field in which men encounter each other in action," and the field is obliterated when *sophia* becomes certain knowledge and *praxis* becomes making or producing. Thus, he argues and concludes that Hayek's critique of constructivism provides a necessary diagnosis of a modern disposition and is a "step toward the emergence of politics from ideological eclipse."

Moulakis is concerned with the second derailment of the *sophia-praxis* relationship, that is, the modern view that *praxis* is devoid of any connection with *sophia*. This is a conception of *praxis* derived from the primordial level of activity: labor and work. There is in modern culture, Moulakis asserts, a pervasive glorification of work, at least in the sense that work purportedly supplies the essential meaning to human life. The emergence of this modern conception of *praxis* as work-activity is traced, starting with the classical view of *praxis* as found in Aristotle. Here *praxis* is understood as "a manner of life qualified and informed by philosophy." Through the Stoics, St. Benedict, Descartes, Hegel, and Marx, Moulakis delineates the threads that are finally woven into the motif that work-activity is the highest mode of *praxis* and the essential activity of man. *Praxis* understood as the glorification of work, Moulakis makes evident, is ethically incoherent as a way of life. *Sophia* is required.

Jurgen Gebhardt

The Origins of Politics in Ancient Hellas: Old Interpretations and New Perspectives

1

We begin our reflection on politics appropriately with reference to (thereby evincing our reverence for) Aristotle: "It is clear that the *polis* is the most perfectly actualized partnership and that man in its utmost actualization is a *zoon politikon*."[1] While these words were written at the end of the lethal crisis of the classical or citizen-polis, they were honed by necessity from the fundamental experience of the Athenian order perceived as an autonomously acting unit of citizens. They contain the paradigm of man's humanity and its order. The *eu zen* (good life) in polis-existence does not refer simply to the brute fact of man's partnership through necessity with other men, as many moderns seem to think; rather, the citizen-polis provides the social framework for that *public* interaction — the political friendship of noetic (rational) selves — which enables man to grow into a *spoudaios* (mature person) and into the above mentioned "utmost actualization" of man's humanity. It will be argued here, in fact, that the classical reflections on politics were founded on the prior paradigmatic historical existence of the polis.[2] Therefore, reflection on the origins of politics must trace the classical experience of politics to its roots, carefully abstaining from the methodological fallacy of interpreting the origins of politics by means of the later language of politics. Moreover, these reflections are essential for historical understanding of the human condition today.[3] This classical comprehension is the necessary corrective for current common opinion that tends to reduce politics to an opaque flux of power relations in the public domain.[4]

I

JÜRGEN GEBHARDT

Only by attention to the classical emergence of political reflection from the prior paradigm of the polis can we understand that we still live in the structural continuity of the historic experience of differentiated reality. "By explicating the political," as Christian Meier explains, "the Greeks formed the eye of the needle world history had to go through in order to reach modern Europe." The discovery of a realm of being that coincides with the realm of human interaction and culminates in a common or public dimension of activity was the historical event that exposes the very constituent of man's humanity as it partakes of a more comprehensive structured reality. This event made paramount to men the differentiated realm of being and defined politics in terms of the structure of human existence newly perceived as the tension between order and disorder, fullness and want, mortality and immortality, and time and eternity. Under the aegis of *ta anthropina* man became increasingly able to act out the whole range of his existential potential, from libidinous drives to ordering reason. This new experiential mode of the differentiated reality of God, nature, man, and society opened up to man's activities a realm of being (i.e., politics), which enabled Western man to start the enterprise of modern civilization. Naturally, the realm of politics is neither purely secular nor purely sacred. It is the area of "in between" that comprises the two poles of existential experience, time and eternity. However, because the innerworldly pole of earthly existence is more successfully managed, there is tangible public proof of its reality. The other dimension of politics is in contemporary thought constantly denied; it is present only in the various modes of more or less desperate searches for the measure that would guide and structure human activities within a more and more chaotic political realm, but these modes are devoid of the very substance of humanity that had once unfolded in the public realm of society and history.

In this respect, the discovery of politics in the Hellenic polis seems to be of considerable interest. To a certain degree, the reflective remembering of the origins of politics may strengthen our awareness of what politics is all about. Certainly the science of politics of Plato and Aristotle is intrinsically intertwined with the unfolding of the political realm in Hellas, but the two are not the same phenomenon. The science of politics did not come into existence coevally with the realm of politics. It was coeval with the crisis of the Hellenic political culture, which occurred at the time when the political realm was still embedded in the undifferentiated cosmological world and was about to disintegrate under the impact of losing its spiritual dimension in the course of a civilizational growth pursued with imperialist ruthlessness, last but not least by Athens. The differentiating event of politics, discovered in the rather limited spatio-temporal area of the Hellenic poleis, had already touched off, on the one hand, a considerable bulk of institutional, behavioral, and symbolic explications of the immanent structure of the realm of politics. On the other hand, politics had inspired a continuously moving process of differentiating experiences that retrospectively would become the symbolic form of philosophy ranging from Xenophanes, Parmenides, and Heraclitus to Plato and Aristotle. To put my argument most pointedly: Mankind explicates its humanity in the course of history, and thus this permanent step in the symbolic self-explication of mankind's humanity, philosophy, originated in politics. The Sophists as well as Plato and Aristotle participated in this movement of consciousness toward the differentiation of reality, unfolding the experiences of this movement in a paradigmatic symbolism of representative humanity. They created political philsophy—the discursive presentation of rational (noetic) acts, acts of thought concerning the order of man in society and history. This achievement raised the first historical experience of the realm of politics to a level of importance that transcended the original spatio-temporal social order of its origins. Although the polis-civilization was historically all but wiped out, its experience continued the process of Western civilization.

To support this thesis I will begin with an analysis of the central philosophical terms, *sophia* and *theoria*. Herodotus's use of these terms is instructive: "There came to Sardis all the Sophists from Hellas who then lived in this or that manner, and among them came Solon the Athenian man *(aner Athenaios),* he having made the laws for the Athenians at their request, left his home for ten years setting out on a voyage, as he said, for the sake of *theoria*," to see the world. After having led Solon around among his treasures, Croisos addressed him: "Our Athenian guest, we have heard much of you by reason of your *sophia* and your wanderings, how you have wandered around the whole world for the sake of *theoria* as somebody who philosophizes *(philosopheon)*."[5] *Theoria, sophia,* and *philosopheon,* in this context, are not technical terms in any respect; they are words of the common parlance among educated people. Yet, there is a meaning implied that points to the specific quality of the emerging self-understanding of the Hellenic culture and that relates, through the reference to Solon as the Athenian lawgiver, philosophizing to the ordering experience of the beginning of the sixth century.

This ordering experience evolved from the crisis of the aristocratic archaic polis and brought forth, in the long run, the very *nomos* of the Hellenic polis, "which has the fairest of all names, *isonomia*." The management of public affairs was made common, and power was given to the people because "there is the whole in the majority."[6] Herodotus has Demaratus, the exiled king of Sparta, describe the *politikon* of the Greeks to Xerxes, who wanted some information about the military quality of his enemy: "By use of *arete* (excellence)," Demaratus says, "Hellas defends herself from poverty and despotism," and *"arete* comes of their own seeking, the fruit of *sophia* and strong *nomos*."[7] The *nomos* of the polis is set against the *nomos* of the Persian despots who rule their subjects by means of the whip while the free Greeks are only afraid of one *despotes,* the law *(nomos)*.[8] Thus, Herodotus traces the great struggle between the Hellenes and the Barbarians, in the last analysis, to their antagonistic ways of life, the Hellenic one being the life of the polis, *to politikon*.[9]

When Pericles, at the height of Athenian greatness, claims in his eulogy "that our polis as a whole is the school of Hellas," he extols the general involvement in *ta politika*. "You will find united in the same persons an interest at once in private matters *(oikeia)* as well as in politics *(ta politika),* and in others of us who give attention chiefly to business, there is no lack of insight into *ta politika.*" This was preceded by the fundamental statement: "For we all are acquiring beauty *(philokaloumen)* with no extravagance and are acquiring knowledge *(philosophoumen)* without effeminacy."[10] Wolfgang Schadewaldt calls this statement the quintessence of what the Athenians meant by culture. Because the acquisition of beautiful things might lead to pomp and ostentation, which is barbaric, Pericles adds: in austerity. Because knowledge and refinement might lead to decadence and mannerisms, he also adds: without effeminacy. Philosophizing in the everyday language of the educated Greek of the fifth century means being directed to tend to the pursuit of knowledge.[11] But a *philosopheon* was always a Greek, never a Barbarian. At first it was Solon, the lawgiver, and finally it was every Athenian citizen living within the historical and geographical boundaries of his *nomos.*

What kind of knowledgeable man was the *sophos* in early times? The *sophos* was a man highly skilled in doing particularly difficult things. A helmsman, for example, might have been a *sophos,* since he exercised his skill in the most dangerous and unexpected circumstances and had to rely on his own capacities. Pindar, the contemporary of Herodotus, distinguished between the *mathontes* who have learned something and the *sophos* who has knowledge of inner growth, that is, a knowledge rooted in the *physis (phya)* of man. The original meaning of a more practical wisdom grounded in some personal or existential knowledge comes from the formative years of the classical citizen-polis, around 550 B.C. The important historical figures who lived around 600 B.C. were canonized as the seven *sophoi.* These lists of names varied, and all the lists combined speak of seventeen wise men. But four men were on each list: the lawgiver Solon of Athens, Pittakos of Mytilene, the wise judge Bias of Priene, and Thales of Miletos. Periander of Corinth, Cheilon of Sparta, and Kleobulos of Lindos were also often named. Practical wisdom and success in politics obviously qualified one to be called a *sophos* and gave evidence of the emergence of the new spiritual and social order of the polis.[12] The *sophos* represents the new panhellenic experience of politics. These were founding fathers of the new polis, and their *sophia* embodies the new knowledge of an ordered polis within the boundaries of the comprehensive order of the cosmos. Their *dicta* refer us to the *delphika parangelmata* (commands), the *gnothi seauton* (know thyself) implies the *thneton onta* (being mortal), and the *thneta phronein* (reflect on the mortal) alerts one to the *metron ariston* (best measure), which commands: *sophronei* (be prudent). The *anthropina* of the recently discovered realm of *ta politika* materialize under the horizon of Apollo, the God of Delphi. As Schadewaldt explains:

> Only the awareness of his mortality as demanded by the God of Delphi offers man the universal norm, the fundamental knowledge and, so to speak, the standard meter by which all other measures of the human are gauged. And thus, within the boundaries of the self-limitations of his mortality and the fixed distance from the divine, man is able to be truly man and to set free his strength to realize his dignity within the range of his potential for freedom and personality.[13]

It is not surprising that the origin of the word *theoria* fits perfectly with this understanding of *sophia* and *sophon*. Solon of Herodotus, to reiterate, was not only a *philosopheon* but also traveled for the sake of *theoria;* that is, he did it in order to watch things in a truly free way without any practical purposes.[14] Schadewaldt contends that the original meaning of *theoria* was "being aware of a god" rather than "being aware of a vision" inasmuch as the word occurred within the context of early Hellenic politics. The *theoros* was the envoy of a polis sent to the sacral festival in other poleis either to consult an oracle or simply to participate in the ritual act by just being present. *Theoria* occurs when the sacral legation observes rituals performed for the respective god. Since the *theoros* was to witness the sacred acts, his presence and observance obtained a spiritual meaning. Thus, *theoria* is not so much a mode of intellectual activity as it is a specific mode of spiritual activity: an "observer partaking in such a sacral-festive event."[15] Since these delegations had to travel all over the known world, *theoria* acquired the meaning of a specific mode of contemplating objects as a *philosopheon*. The evidence is therefore strong that *sophia* and *theoria,* the central tenets of the symbolic form of

Hellenic *philosophia,* are grounded in the experiential world of the *présence civique,* the new order of the citizen-polis.

The contours of this unfolding of the classical experience of politics might be outlined as follows: In the Achean kingdoms of Homer the word *polis* circumscribes only a dwelling of people ruled by the nobles of the realm. In the archaic society, the polis was not an acting partner in the symbolic drama of order and disorder as told by the poet.[16] Nor does Hesiod's mytho-poetic explication of an incipient human condition reflect any primacy to the polis in locating the forces of order and disorder. Order *(eunomia),* Justice *(dike),* and Peace *(eirene),* the daughters of Zeus, operate in the Olympic realm of *Cosmos* and *Chaos* and are engaged in the titanic struggle against the forces of disorder *(dysnomia)* and against her sisters such as misery, war, and hunger. Among the mortal men of the polis, *eunomia* springs from the ethical personality of reigning Zeus. Human actions and sufferings appear as a distinctive dimension of the Olympic world. The Jovian order, on the other hand, always knows about the injustice and hubris of the powerful in the polis, as measured against the ethical forces of *eunomia.* The "I Hesiod" is the mortal speaking out as a man who conceives of the unjust actions of the powerful, the corruptibility of the judges, and the expropriation and oppression of the peasants as *dysnomia* in the Olympian context. However, the polis proper was not yet differentiated in terms of a realm of being determined by the interaction of ethical forces and counterforces in the lives of men. The *nomos,* which appears in Hesiod for the first time, is the Zeus-given order of living beings, and *dike* is the principle of the *nomos* of men as distinguished from the *nomos* of animals bound to eat each other. But the *eunomia* and the *dysnomia* do not yet refer to the state of affairs of the polis, that is, the *nomos* of the community.[17]

The epics of Homer and Hesiod, written between 730 and 700 B.C., tell us about the archaic aristocratic polis. It emerged from the context of tribally organized people *(ethnos)* during the course of the eighth century and developed into an autonomous political and economic unit in Ionia, on the islands of the Aegean, and in the eastern districts of the Greek mainland.

7

The erosion of the sacred kingship brought forth these aristocratic units. They were based upon a gentilitian structure and
grew into communities that concentrated all major activities
within their territorial bounds. Thus, the polis meant a socioreligious center for little agrarian societies in which the aristocratic families shared power over the multitude of landowning
peasants. However, the social and economic differences among
the elites and the masses remained rather small. The absence
of any imperial pressure from the outside or from within induced the prosperous elite to test the open horizon of the Aegean
world. Overseas pillage, long-distance trade, and foreign military service merged into the movement of colonization that,
from the middle of the eighth century until the sixth century,
expanded the polis-culture from the Black Sea to the French
and Italian coasts. Finally, in addition to the 200 poleis in the
Aegean, some 2300 more independent polis-societies were started.[18]

The unifying experience of this civilizational process was
provided by the fabric of an overarching aristocratic culture rooted in the spiritual authority of such religious centers as the
Oracle of Delphi. These centers of panhellenic consciousness
furnished, by means of the newly developed alphabet, a communicative unity for the poly-political system of the Greeks,
and they also became a source of ordering knowledge that
would supply the order of the *nomos* in a time when the self-
evidence of the aristocratic way of life was to lose its grip on
the polis-society. Hesiod's concern with the right order already
echoes the crisis of the aristocratic society of archaic Greece.

"Colonization, mercenary service, and internal stresses,"
Chester Starr concludes, "were all interwoven manifestations
of the great alterations in the Greek world in the eighth and
following centuries."[19] Trade, piracy, and colonization were carried on by many poleis. There were so many single persons,
families, groups, and even enterprising nonaristocrats involved
in these ventures that the benefits of riches, power, and reputa-
tion were shared among subjects. In fact, neither monarchs nor
a few powerful lords were able to monopolize the fruit of ex-
pansion for the purpose of the formation of centralized power

8

units. The new horizons of action, experiences, and knowledge were widely spread among a broad spectrum of social groups on the move.[20] The crisis of the old society seemed to be induced by the dynamics of civilizational growth: Rural change occurred with the rise of middling farmers into the upper class; the factionalization of the aristocracy developed; the genesis of the new type of military, the hoplites, and of new technologies that spurred trade and industry occurred; finally, after 600 B.C., the appearance of coinage changed the internal structure of the polis, weakened the gentilitian organization, and fostered an urbanization that redefined the modes of the religious and political focus of the polis.

The destruction of the archaic substratum of the social life caused misery, indebtedness, and enslavement for certain segments of the peasants. It destabilized both the social relations between lords and peasants and the power relations within the polis and between the poleis, and it invited strong men to seize power and establish a new kind of one-man-rule, tyranny.[21] Meier argues that this fundamental crisis might have led to a monarchic consolidation of the social order modeled on the near-eastern empires, or it might have developed into a modified aristocratic order as happened in Rome. But, from the Hellenic configuration, there resulted the epochal event of politics: With the weakness of monarchy and aristocracy, with the social mobility of semiaristocrats and middling farmers, and with the exploitation of the lower classes by tyrannical adventurers, the field of social interaction was expanded and provided new modes of social integration.[22] The dislocation of the old order provided to the *sophoi,* who represent the panhellenic spirituality of the God of Delphi, the opportunity for the social embodiment of those experiences of order that adhere to the quest for *eunomia.* Transcending the singularity of the respective poleis, this intellectual and religious movement anticipated a consciousness of the polis that was modeled on the *sophia* of the *sophoi,* the personal spiritual experiences of the *ta anthropina* to be acted upon according to the measure of the God. The consciousness could respond to the social doubts about the merit of the old *nomos* of the polis by reflecting on the condition of the *nomos* itself. The *sophoi* thus were able to reformulate for members of the polis the principles of right conduct, which were so much in doubt in a time of crisis and confusion.[23]

Homer and Hesiod had already searched for the excellence of their men and found it in the *arete,* respectively, of the aristocratic warrior and the peasant. Snell and, particularly, Schadewaldt emphasize that the poet's *agathon* (Homer) or *arete* (Hesiod) points at a reflexive quest for the good itself: "the being itself or something as ordained by the overarching order of the cosmos."[24] *Arete* of men, therefore, was from the beginning bound up with the best way of living together, which was *dikaiosyne.*[25] The destruction of the archaic world of the old poets is evinced by the poetry of the seventh century. Archilochos (680-640 B.C.), the aristocratic hoplite for hire, as well as Sappho (600 B.C.) or Mimnermos (600 B.C.), tell us about the experiences of individuals set free from the archaic ethos and involved in a futile search for the best within man himself.[26] On mainland Greece, however, the quest discovered the new *arete,* not in the ethos of the aristocrat or the peasant but in the right participation within the *nomos* of the polis. This experience gave the old and new groups, emerging from the institutional and socioeconomic framework of the crisis-ridden polis, a new sense of community. To be *Athenaioi* meant to extend the *koinon* to a demos, that is, to make it a *demosion,* and thereby bind the new social substratum of peasants, artisans, traders, and old aristocrats into a collectively acting citizenry. Thus, the polis had to be experienced as more than an external fabric within a wider cosmic reality.[27] As Voegelin explains, the new "pathos of the polis was the pathos of a dynamic participation of the people in a culture that originated in the aristocratic society. The dynamics was on the side of the 'people' " absorbing the new differentiated truth of humanity and offering a new self-understanding in a changed social situation.[28]

The history of Athens from Solon to Peisistratos and Cleisthenes is the paradigmatic case study of this encounter, which extended, moreover, over the whole of the Hellenic civilization. Before Solon, the *nomos* of a polis implied the mores and rules as the given form of the aristocratic society. There were *nomoi* of different poleis, but such differences were not a matter of principles of order. Complaints about the state of the *nomos* were made only matter-of-factly; disorder could not be conceived of in terms of ordering experiences, which would allow a judgment about the state of affairs in a polis. The discovery of politics implies becoming aware of an inherent principle of community in order to interpret social states of order and disorder. This is Solon's concept of *eunomia;* he "makes it the principal cause of the good condition of the polis."[29] This principle of right order was to integrate the multitude of quarreling inhabitants into the polis with a novel political existence. In 594 B.C. the aristocrat Solon was called in as *diallaktes* in order to mediate between the warring factions of the society. In doing so, Solon not only accepted the landed aristocracy as participants of the common culture of action but admitted also other sections of the society into this common order of the polis, which had ceased to be a culture of the old aristocratic society. The pathos of the polis grew out of the dynamics of public action of different social groups, old and new elites, as well as middling farmers, united in a newly discovered realm of common interest, the *demosion,* that is, politics. There the questions of order and disorder, *eunomia* and *dysnomia,* involved the conduct of men themselves. "Solon has discovered," Meier points out, "that in the polis of his time certain events . . . take place in a socially immanent context of cause and effect. . . ."[30] Similarly, Voegelin argues that for the first time the historico-political process appears as a chain of cause and effect; human action is the cause of order or disorder in the polis.[31] Voegelin hints also at the Ionian Physicists reflecting on the source of this new aitiology and quotes Solon: "From the cloud comes the strength of snow and hail, and thunder is born from bright lightning; a polis is ruined by its great men, and the people fall into servitude of a tyranny through its simplemindedness."[32] This text is not a case of filiation but proves again the general Hellenic experiential complex of the search for the ordering measure discovering the in-itself of things and men.

In the elegy *Our Polis,* which was written before he became *archon,* Solon sketches out the picture of disorder, putting the singular events of misdemeanor into one coherent frame of reference:

> This is a wound that cometh inevitable and forthwith to every city, and she falleth quickly into an evil servitude, which arouseth discord and waketh slumbering War that destroyeth the lovely prime of so many men. . . . Such are the evils which then are rife among the common folk, and many of the poor go slaves into a foreign land, bound with unseemly fetters, there to bear perforce the evil works of servitude. So cometh the common evil into every house, and the street-doors will no longer keep it out; it leapeth the high hedge and findeth every man, for all he may go hide himself in his chamber.

Athens has not heeded the "awful foundation of *dike,* who is so well aware in her silence of what is and what has been, and soon or late comes always to avenge." But Athens will not perish by the will of the gods, but "her own inhabitants *(astoi)* for lucre's sake, are fain to make ruin of this great polis by their folly."[33] Not the gods, but the actions of men are responsible for the miserable state of polis-affairs. Later, in the face of the tyranny of Peisistratos, Solon tells his fellow citizens: "If you suffer through your own fault, blame you not the Gods for it; for yourselves you have exalted these men by giving them guards (or pledges), and therefore it is that you enjoy foul servitude."[34]

The ordering force of the *dike* of Zeus threatens the responsible evildoers with punishment if they do not revert to order, to *eunomia.* Solon's discovery of lawlike cause-and-effect relationships governing social processes is tied to the firm conviction that the citizens are able to turn the fate of the society for the better. "The insight into the inevitability of the general evil made it possible to prevent its coming," according to Meier.[35] From this insight into the pattern of responsible human action, Solon concludes:

> This it is that my heart *(thymos)* bids me to tell the Athenians, and how that even as *dysnomia* gives a polis much trouble, so *eunomia* makes all things orderly *(eukosma)* and perfect *(artia),* and often puts fetters on the unrighteous; and she makes the rough smooth, checks hubris, confuses outrage; she withers the springing weeds of ruin, she straightens crooked judgments,

she mollifies proud deeds; she stops the work of faction, she stills the wrath of baneful strife; and by her all relating to men is made well-ordered *(artia)* and proper *(pinyta).*[36]

Solon links his awareness of the presence of ordering *dike* in the realm of social action with the understanding of human responsibility for these very actions. Man (i.e., Solon the law-giver) is called to respond to *dike* by the restoration of *eunomia*. The *eunomia* of the polis rises from the *eunomia* of the *thymos* (heart) of Solon by the means of his laws. "Why did I stay me ere I had won that for which I gathered the *demos*?" The indentured are free again, as are the enslaved; those sold abroad or exiled are also freed. "By fitting close together right and might I made these things prevail, and accomplished them even as I said I would. And ordinances *(thesmoi)* I wrote, that made straight justice *(dike)* for each man, good and bad alike."[37] This was done amid heavy social conflicts. Different social factions expected Solon to side with them. He had to disappoint his fellow aristocrats, as well as those who desired an equal share in land for everybody. "I stood with a strong shield thrown before both sorts, and would have neither to prevail unrighteously over the other."[38] Solon enacted for the first time the citizens' responsibility for the *koinon* of the polis. "What was achieved by this, is difficult to imagine today. . . . The realm of politics (the concerns of the polis-society) is dissociated from the realm of the surrounding nature. . . . The fate of the polis is, on the other hand, principally separated from the fate of the individual mortal," which is as incalculable as ever.[39] This realm of politics is privileged insofar as the gods, in the case of Athens, the daughter of Zeus, Athene, "hold their hands over us," as Solon maintains. By the favor of the divine, the polis is free to choose between *dysnomia* and *eunomia*.

Politics, in the sense of an autonomous realm of human actions, requires a new definition of the man best suited to act in this realm. The excellences of the old aristocracy are still highly esteemed by Solon. But under the conditions of the times they easily deteriorate, and there is suppression and exploitation of the people. The same holds true for the excellence of the wealthy newcomers. The new excellence of the polis, *arete,* is not to be determined by social status: "Many bad men are rich, many good men are poor; but we will not exchange *arete* for these men's wealth, for *arete* lasts forever while possessions are in the hand of one man, then another."[40] Ever since the discovery of politics the quest for the true *arete* of the citizen-men has been decisive and crucial to all politics. The Solonian quest is not answered by sampling the current opinions people have about themselves, because the *arete* of man is not grounded in the illusionary opinions of men about their respective life goals, their needs, or their wants: "We mortal men, alike good and bad, are minded *(noeumen)* thus: each of us keeps the *doxa* (opinion) he has ever had till he suffers ill, and then forthwith he grieves." The sick hope to be healthy, the poor to be rich, the cowards to be brave, and the ugly man to be good-looking. All men of whatever business or profession pursue their worldly aims and strive for the fulfillment of their desires and needs. But worldly success is not at the disposal of men but is meted out by Fate *(moira)*. This pursuit of social achievements, particularly the drive for riches, is in itself without any purpose, "for the richest among us are twice as eager to have more than others, and who can satisfy all?"[41] We have seen that *dysnomia* springs up when the realm of human action is governed by the unfettered pursuit of power and riches, and that it is induced by *doxa,* the illusions of man about himself. *Eunomia* requires that man must renounce his *doxa* in order to revert to the true springs of action, the *arete* of the citizen-man.

In Solon, the contours of this new *arete* of politics appear in history for the first time. The civilizational unfolding of the polis-society in Athens called for a new excellence of its members, which, once practiced, would bring about *eunomia*. The *arete,* as Voegelin explains, cannot consist in the possession of finite goods: "The goods at which man aims through his action are apparent only; they belong to the *doxa* of wishes and pursuits."[42] This *arete* is different from the archaic codices of conduct. The new excellence requires the existential self-formation of the citizen-man, which must be open to the ordering experience of the *gnothi seauton* as paradigmatically explicated by the *sophos,* Solon: "It is very hard to apperceive the unseen measure of right knowledge (*gnomosyne,* right judgment) in thinking vision *(noesai),* and yet it alone contains the right boundaries *(peirata)* of all things."[43] The true *arete* is actualized in the process of becoming aware of the source of order, which in itself is beyond the world of tangible things. This is called *noein;* we watch the emergence of *nous* (intellect or reason) as the constitutive force moving man to the search for his humanity and its order. Solon knows: "The *nous* of the immortals is all unseen to men,"[44] but man is also able to transcend *doxa* in conforming with the unseen measure. Solon is the model: "At the behest of the Gods have I done what I said."[45] The experiential core of the new *arete* of the citizen-man is the existential tension between the disordering forces of the life of *doxa* (the needs, passions, and drives of the individuals) and the ordering force of the unseen measure that unites the citizens in the common realm of good actions, that is, politics.

This Solonian exploration of the problems of order articulated the new reflexive self-consciousness of an intellectual movement in the polis-world, which, as Meier claims, was rooted in the religious realism of Delphi. From this intellectual movement emerged a position that explicated an experience of true order within the social and institutional framework of the polis but beyond the warring factions: "It contained a nucleus of crystallization around which the solidarity, the judgment, and the unified political will of large sections of the population . . . could be formed."[46] At the time of the crises of the old aristocratic and the new tyrannical regimes, this reflection in self-consciousness conceived of a community of new citizen-men, and it anticipated a polis-order grounded in a new social substratum and consisting of individual members of the polis-society. It prepared the way toward the social embodiment of the new experience of order as well. Meier calls it a time of a "revaluation of values" in favor of a more polis-related ethics: "Wisdom and justice could appear as the most important virtues. And this was congruent with the demands of larger sections of the populations for justice *(dike).*"[47]

The Solonian break with the archaic view is clearly seen when contrasted with the more conventional aristocratic reaction to the social and spiritual crisis of the sixth century. This reaction is found in the collection of elegaic poems preserved under the name of Theognis of Megara.[48] The poems carry a running argument with Solon, quoting extensively from his elegies. But Theognis turns the Solonian critique of the polis into a factional manifesto of the declining aristocracy.[49] He denies any human responsibility for common action, and he sets against the ordering experience of the unseen measure the inconceivable acts of the old gods. From these acts, Theognis maintains, no *eunomia* will spring up in the polis; there will be no common world of the *demosion;* there will be no binding together of the old aristocracy, the *nouveaux riches,* and the farming multitude; and there will be only perplexity *(amechania)* among all of them:

> No one is himself the cause of his disaster or gain. No: the gods are the givers of both these things to men. Nor does any man know as he works whether he is making for an *agathon* or a *kakon* goal. For often when he thinks he will bring about an *esthlon* end, he brings about a *kakon*. Nor does any man gain what he wishes; for the constraints of dire perplexity *(amechania)* have him in their grasp. Vain are the practices of us mortal men, for we know nothing, but the gods accomplish all things in accordance with their *noos.*[50]

Theognis formulated an anti-Solonian position based upon the traditional aristocratic code of conduct, which was threatened by the rise of new classes to power. The Theognis argument is quite plausible in view of the author's social situation, but it would have never led to to the discovery of politics. The Solonian *eunomia* is grounded in a new experience of order that will provide the social complex of the polis with the new understanding of a community of citizens acting according to the excellence of the citizen, as guided by the unseen measure. In this respect, Solon represents the independent social authority of a "third position," institutionalizing the interest in the polis as a whole beyond the warring factions of the Hellenic poleis.

This authority, Meier claims, sets the political goals in response to the discontent and sensitivity of the citizenry, which it had helped to arouse in the first place.[51] The quest for the true order of existence within the institutional framework of the polis, that is, *eunomia,* initiated a process toward the *isonomia* of the reforms of Cleisthenes and, according to Starr, broke the ground for the Athenian paradigm of classical democracy: "By the late seventh and sixth centuries the Greek world had achieved a variety of modes by which to release or appease its fundamental uncertainties and had established a new religious and psychological base for an active existence."[52] This base resulted from the highly complicated interplay of the new forces of spiritual authority and the manifold social and economic determinants of the civilizational process, which Meier and his students call the politicization of the polis-society: "By 'politicization,' the change is to be understood which was brought about by comprehending a social world materializing among citizens, i.e., becoming political."[53] This civilizational process of polis-formation stretched over the Greek world from Sicily to Anatolia and from Macedonia to North Africa. But it was neither uniform nor continuous, and the Persian conquest of the poleis in Asia Minor in 546 B.C. moved the focus of the development to the West.

It is important to stress the fact that the policy of the early tyranny—still the topic of much heated scholarly debate—facilitated the social integration of the polis-society and incorporated the different strands of new spiritual and religious experiences into the framework of the polis. This policy paved the way for the social embodiment of the spiritual substance of *virtue* within the citizen-polis. It has been rightly argued, therefore, that tyranny contributed to the politicization of the religious life of the polis.[54]

Jaeger was well aware of the political implications of the new religious forces engendered by the resurgent archaic mystery cults, Orphism in Greece and the related Pythagorean movement in Italy. He states that "the sixth century meant for Greece a renewal of the religious life to be linked to the social crisis of the polis." In particular, he points out that the "social and political rise of the lower classes was accompanied also by the penetration of their religious conceptions into the higher intellectual life, thus smoothing the way for decisive changes."[55] The cult of Dionysus now came to be held in mounting esteem and was to find a place in the public festivals and divine ceremonies of the poleis of Sicyon under Cleisthenes, Corinth under Periander, and Athens under the Peisistratidae. The dithryamb and Attic tragedy and comedy owe their origin to these ceremonies. "Hand in hand with the rise of the cult of Dionysus went a revival of the ancient local mysteries, which were favored by much the same political forces."[56] Peisistratus built the new Telesterion at Eleusis, investing the cult of Eleusis with new significance for the public life of the city. Even if we agree with Nilsson that there was no specific religious policy of the tyrants, we have to keep in mind that the Peisistratidae achieved the religious-cultural unification of Attica.[57] They forced back the aristocratic gentilitian cults and the cults of local gods in favor of a centralized polis cult of Athenae and united all citizens in the public feast of the Panathenaia. They also introduced the panhellenic gods for devotion. But even more important, they opened the polis to the rejuvenated archaic religious cults of the populace. Before too long the esoteric and exoteric ways of the new spirituality of the citizen-man penetrated Athens. In the citizen-man the Delphic religion of Apollo and the ecstatic experiences of the new nongentilitian cult communities meet and bring forth the new modes of cultural life that determined the political identity of the polis.

The crucial elements for my understanding of the politicization of the religious life are these: The discovery of politics refers, on the one hand, to the personal formation of the new excellence of the citizen by means of the quest for and experience of the unseen measure and, on the other hand, to the public presentation of the newly discovered common humanity of the citizen-man in the festivals of the polis. If the realm of politics is constituted by the social interaction of the self-responsible citizen-man, then, the ordering experience of the formation of the citizen-man's new excellence must constitute the authentic self of the citizen-man and must delineate the area of the experiences of order and disorder within one's own existence. This realm of one's own identity was to be called *psyche*. The discovery of politics, I suggest, involves the discovery of the psyche.

In the face of the scanty material, as well as the divers interpretations about the discovery of the soul in the course of the politicization of the polis, one can only lay claim to a plausibility that rests to a certain degree on the subsequent presence of the newly discovered humanity of the soul and its order in the mystic philosophers of the polis in the fifth and fourth centuries. Voegelin, for example, reasons: "The conception of the immortal soul, of its origin, fall, wanderings, and ultimate bliss . . . must be presupposed in the thinkers of the generation around 500 B.C. In particular, it must be presupposed in Heraclitus who consciously explores the dimensions of this soul."[58]

The new posthomeric meaning of the word *psyche* materializes in new religious modes of polis life. The Homeric *psyche* was an impersonal life force that departed from man in death and joined the shades in Hades, while *thymos* designated the "personal" in man, which died with him. In the ecstatic experiences of the new cult communities the citizen-man encounters the divine in him, which brings forth a new self-understanding; life and spirit merge into a unit constituting the "permanence of a person." According to Jaeger, the *psyche* "as a spiritual being in its own right, quite independent of the corporeal," preserves its identity both before and after this life.[59] This is expressed in the Orphic and Pythagorean ideas of *metempsychosis,* the transmigration of the soul.

The discovery of the soul involves three interrelated items: First, the new term *empsychon* designates the living being and *psyche* is in it. Burkert states that "something individual and permanent is contained in living beings, whether they are men or animals. It is an 'I' preserving its identity due to its own essence and independently from the body which dissolves. . . . Death does not affect this *psyche:* the soul is immortal, *Athanatos.*"[60] Schadewaldt makes the crucial point: It is novel that the personality of man was located in the soul and, consequently, that the body was conceived as the prison or the tomb of the soul. It is the soul of man that represents his true humanity and is the indestructible source of all experience of reality and truth *(aletheia).*[61] Second, the orphic conception of the immortal soul, comprising the personality and individuality of man, has an important bearing on the conduct of the citizen-man. It reenforces "the person as an intellectually and morally responsible agent, actively cooperating in his own fate, though immersed in the general natural processes of coming-to-be and passing-away to which even man seems irresistibly subjected."[62] There is still the traditional notion of Hades, but the permanence of the truly human in man after death is emphasized. The earlier ideas of the judgment of the dead, of punishments and rewards, gain a new relevance. The dead have to answer for their *bios* (life).[63] The *Elysium* of the blessed is the place for souls who have lead a pure life; man is burdened with the responsibility for the future fate of his *psyche* "whether he expects to obtain his salvation by mere adherence to outward rituals or rather by some ethical sanctification in the course of his wanderings."[64] The man who experiences the immortal in himself by way of the ecstatic rituals of the new social communities is the citizen-man in search of his new *arete,* which brings about *eunomia* by responsible action in the common realm of politics. Hence, the *thymos* of Solon, the sensorium of the unseen measure, was now called *psyche,* denoting the presence of ordering forces of *dike* in all citizen-men. This *psyche* bestowed upon them a common humanity, that is, the core of the *présence civique* initiated by the reforms of Cleisthenes in Athens.

In this respect, the equality of the *isonomia*—the political equipoise of the old aristocracy and the rising forces of the people—meant to establish *eunomia* among the free citizens: The *nomos* of the well-ordered polis rules where the *demos* rules insofar as the management of public affairs was made common by way of *isogoria,* which is synonymous with *isonomia. Isonomia* is first of all opposed to tyranny. The term "makes its earliest appearance as an adjective in the famous drinking-song of Harmodios and Aristogeiton," at the time of the reforms of Cleisthenes. The song praised the two tyrannicides "because they have killed the tyrant and made Athens *isonomous.*"[65] This *isonomous* order was the answer to the hubris, the license, and the ill-will of the tyrant's rule. Hence, *isonomia* denoted not only the equal share of the citizens in the political realm but was rooted, as Meier claims, in the "original conception of equality in terms of justice and the assurance of the absence of license."[66] Knauss states that "it is only from *dikaiosyne* that the *nomos* can permanently materialize; it becomes, therefore, the most important citizen-virtue, the specific *arete politike*."[67] Finally, as Gregory Vlastos explains, *isonomia* implied *eunomia*: "It designates . . . not a specific constitution but a standard by which constitutions can be evaluated."[68]

Within the polis of the fifth century the differentiated experience of *ta politika* brought forth the new understanding of the arrangement of governmental powers among the citizenry and within the framework of *isonomia*. Different *nomoi* could be distinguished once the *demos* held power in a polis. The new political terms of the fifth century (democracy, oligarchy, monarchy, and other related terms) indicate "that fundamental, decisive distinctions between polis-orders were made in terms of rulership. At least it has become known very soon, that the matter of rulership was the decisive property of constitutions."[69] Once the *isonomia* was understood in terms of rulership *(arche)* and power *(kratos),* the institutional organization of the polis-order came into focus. The share of the citizens in the political partnership became a matter of institutional arrangement, the *politeia* of the polis. This new term for the institutional complex of polis-order came into existence in the late fifth century. At first in Herodotus it meant the right of being a citizen; later, the meaning expanded to the whole of the citizenry and public life in general. Around 430 B.C., according to Meier, the meaning of citizenry and constitutional order merge: "The reason for the formation and acceptance of this novel concept of constitution might, in the last analysis, be traced to the insight that . . . the composition and the demarcation of the citizenry decided upon the constitution of the city."[70] Thus, the process of politicization has culminated in this idea of *politeia*: "In it the identity between citizenry and polis is attained."[71] But the old measure of good order holds true for *politeia* as well, in that it is not the lust for power and honors that make *arche* and *kratos* political but their reference to *nomos* and *dike*.

The discovery of the soul under the experiential horizon of politics differentiated the Delphic humanity of Solon: The ordering force of *dike* emerges from the depth of the human soul and attunes the newly discovered humanity of the responsible and mature citizen-man to the ordered whole of reality, which embraces the polis as well as the cosmos. This is the third aspect of the discovery of the soul. In lecturing about the Pythagorean myth of the soul, Schadewaldt remarks that this experience of the soul, as the vehicle of man's humanity, "opened the door to a new realm of being." He continues, "now being is not anymore the existent," the *onta* of things and men; "the soul is not existent in this sense and tangible, and yet there is more being *(mehr seinsartig)* to it than to the existent." This new area of the soul opened up spiritual reality for the search of "the grounds of the existent."[72] In his "Homer's View of Man" Snell relies on Heraclitus and the lyric poets to explore this "opening up" of the new realm of being. His remarks clarify Schadewaldt's argument: "The notion of the depth of the soul . . . is designed to throw light on the outstanding trait of the soul and its realm: that it has its own dimension, that is not extended in space. . . . The soul, as contrasted with things physical, reaches into infinity." The lyric poets were the first "to voice this new idea that intellectual and spiritual matters have 'depth.' " "The symbol of depth always points to the infinity of the intellectual and spiritual which differentiate it from the physical."[73]

This experience of the soul and its order became the motivating force in the new symbolic modes that expressed the newly differentiated humanity of the citizen-man. The new symbolisms expanded the common partnership in public action from the order of the soul (now the experiential center of order) into the order of the cosmos, thus making man an actor playing a part in the drama of being. Accordingly, the Solonian quest for *eunomia* and its unseen measure is restated in terms of a divine ground of being more or less radically emancipated from the anthropomorphism of the old world of the gods. Further, the new interpreters of the Hellenic mind can no longer play the Solonian role of the *diallaktes,* the one who takes upon himself the ordering of the polis. The self-responsible citizenry is called to realize *eunomia* on its own. The mystic philosophers and the poets of the Athenian Tragedy ask the citizen-man for reenactment of the new humanity, but on a different plane. The manifold religious, intellectual, and spiritual irruptions within the frame of the panhellenic mind were now firmly grounded in politics, and they merged in the course of the civilizational process of the late fifth and early fourth centuries to bring forth these two world-historic symbolic modes of Hellenic self-interpretation.

The Athenian poets and the mystic philosophers differ in their symbolic response to the experience of the soul and its order. The poets of the tragedy immersed themselves into the civilizational process of Athens and gave meaning to the new politics from Cleisthenes to Pericles of the *présence civique*.[74] The tragedy is the public celebration and interpretation of the citizen-man, and it is the common reenactment of the *koinophiles dianoia* (the spirit of the love of the common) in the citizen-men.[75] The substance of the new isonomic order is found in the political friendship activated in common action and is moved by the pervading force of the Jovian *dike*. This action, expressed and experienced in the tragedy, calls for the actualization of the new humanity in the citizen-men. The spiritual and practical capacity of the citizen-man is called *phronesis* (prudence), the gods' best gift.[76] *Phronesis* means the existential virtue of right, conscious action; it is a specific habit of knowingly realizing the unseen measure in concrete responsible action. In his action the prudent man testifies to the true *logos* of his existence. For Schadewaldt, "this human sense of direction in the area of the *agatha* and *kaka*" activates the divine in man and awakes him to his true stature of citizen-man as required for public action.[77] Acting out *phronesis* provides the community with *sophrosyne*, which, as Snell reports, "was a kind of moral measure, designed to stabilize the harmony of healthy life" and "the concordance of opposites."[78] It keeps the parts of the whole adjusted to each other. In the tragedy the term is polis-related: The prudent man's deliberation and moderation keep the whole of political interaction in equipoise.[79]

The political interpretation of the tragedy is still the subject of much scholarly dispute, but certain plausible insights can be gained from the works of Jaeger, Voegelin, Dodds, and Meier. The tragedy rearranged the symbolic material of the archaic anthropomorphism for the purpose of the religious-cultural life of the citizen-polis. The theomorphic symbols, however, provided the poet "with a divine personnel which could credibly act out the tragedy of the soul." As Voegelin pointed out in his study of *Prometheus,* it is "a study of the forces in the human soul that will create social order when they are properly balanced, and will destroy this order when the balance is destroyed."[80] According to Voegelin, "the truth of the tragedy is action itself, that is, action on the new differentiated level of a movement in the soul that culminates in the decision *(prohairesis)* of a mature responsible man. The newly discovered humanity of the soul expands into the realm of action."[81]

The action in the public realm emanates from the decision making of the human soul, but the whole of the polis participates in this process of decision making. Aeschylus's *Suppliants* are the best proof for this interpretation.[82] Forced to choose between the welfare of the city and the rightful demands of the suppliants, King Pelasgus has to come up with a decision in accordance with *dike.* In this situation he reflects "downward into the depth" of his soul in order to make up his mind. But since the whole *(to koinon)* of the polis is concerned, he states the people will have to find the solution in common *(xyne).* Before the king is to decide he must have communicated *(koinosas)* with the people.[83] "Nothing without the *demos,*" he argues against the chorus.[84] Also, he claims to represent the polis and the *demos.* The case is submitted to the general body *(koinon)* of the citizens, and the king by means of persuasion *(peitho)* convinces them to grant the desired safeguard. It was the Pelasgian people that willingly heard the subtle windings of the speech, but, as Voegelin explains, it was Zeus who brought the end to pass: "The descent into the depth was taken in common and what the people found was the Dike of Zeus."[85]

Tragedy presents the politics of the mature citizen-men, and it represents the public life of the citizen-men. It enacts the representative emergence of *dike* from the depth of the soul, thus illuminating the true meaning and substance of the *présence civique*. Politics itself, as Voegelin insists, "acquires the hue of tragedy when it is understood as the work of man, as an order wrested by man from the demonic forces of disorder, as a precarious incarnation of Dike achieved and preserved by the efforts of tragic action."[86] The poets of the tragedy breathe the spirit of the mystic philosophers who lived well into the time of the early tragedy. But the tragedy was to dissolve at the end of the century when the public realm of the polis started to disintegrate. The spirit of the mystic philosophers, however, was to live in the symbolic form of philosophy that transcended the limits of polis-politics and the citizen-man.

As far as we know, Xenophanes, Pythagoras, Parmenides, and Heraclitus were somehow involved in polis-politics or at least affected by it.[87] They seemed to be eminent figures representing the "free-floating" panhellenic intelligentsia; they absorbed all strands of the rich religious, spiritual, and cultural life that welled up from the new civilizational world of the polis-citizen. They reformulated the position of the free and independent arbiter passing judgment upon all polis concerns. Their personal knowledge was still the public knowledge of the polis-culture even if this was not recognized by fellow citizens. These thinkers claimed the authority to speak out the truth of the *présence civique* against the opinions current in the poleis. They thought in opposition to, or critical distance from, the polis insofar as they held the mirror up to the polis in order to make their fellow citizens see the true order of the polis. This true order is articulated in their knowledge and is derived from their personal experience of truth, which distinguishes the *philosophos,* as Heraclitus says, from the delusions of the rest of the people. In the elegiac poems of Xenophanes this consciousness of order appeals to the polis to recognize her true destiny. He attacks the still-living aristocratic agonal culture that gives to the victor of Olympia the greatest public honor: "And he would not be worthy to have it as I am! For better than the strength of men or horses is our *sophia* (wisdom). Senseless indeed is custom in such matter; it is not right *(dikaion)* to

25

judge strength higher than the most holy *sophia*." Never for a great agonist "would the polis be better in *eunomia*. And little joy would accrue to the polis if a man through his efforts conquer at the banks of Pisa, for that would not fatten storerooms of the polis."[88] *Eunomia* and prosperity of the polis require the public recognition of the new *arete* of the thinking man, that is, the *sophia,* which is rooted in the experience of the divine and is beyond or beneath the anthropomorphic gods of Homer and Hesiod: "There is one god greatest among gods and men, who is like to mortals neither in form nor mind."[89] The socioreligious order of the polis in general needs to be reconstructed in accordance with the new critical standards of *eunomia.*

The quest for the critical measure of truth and untruth is the great theme of Parmenides: The new knowledge of *sophia* is neither the archaic knowledge of tradition nor "subjective" knowledge of the individual but the authoritative knowledge of the citizen-man, who pursues *dike* (justice) and *themis* (law) to the roots of their measure. Citizens are to follow the way of truth: "Meet is it for you to learn all things: the unshaken heart of wellrounded truth *(aletheia)* as well as the delusion *(doxa)* of the mortals in which there is not true reliance at all. And this you will also learn thoroughly—how going through all things one shall discern the delusions *(dokounta).*"[90] The poem explicates the "peak experience," revealed in *noein* (visionary comprehension), of the ordered structure of the immaterial intelligible reality behind the *onta* and the *anthropina.* In consequence of the visionary experience, the *nous* (intellect) and the *logos* (rationally speaking) will determine the true center of the humanity of citizen-man, and that will immortalize him and make him man proper.[91] "The *nous* . . . brings Being into grasp" of man, while "the content of Being is articulated by the *logos*. . . ."[92] In the course of these experiences the contours of a new understanding of the *koinon* materialize. The core of the experience of politics, the common and public realm, is being redefined in terms of the rationality of the citizen-man.

Heraclitus elucidates the new meaning of the public and the common and turns it into a harsh critique of polis-citizens who refuse to be in the presence of their *nous* and their *logos* and who thereby miss their obligation to the public order of the polis. Heraclitus insists: "It concerns all men to know themselves and to understand *(phronein)*."[93] It is the duty for men to "follow the common. But though the *logos* is common, the many live as if they have *phronesis* of their own."[94] The true meaning of the public and private dimensions of politics comes into focus: "Those who are awake have a world *(kosmos)*, one and common, but those who are asleep turn aside into their private *(idion)* worlds."[95] "It is not meet to act and speak like men asleep," he states.[96] The *logos* creates the public partnership in the realm of prudential interaction. In the end, however, the *logos* of public speech and public action is grounded in the public *nous* of man partaking in the universal order of the whole of reality: "Those who speak with *nous* must strengthen themselves with that which is common to all as the polis does with the law and more strongly so. For all human laws nourish themselves from the one divine; for this holds sway as far as it will, and suffices for all, and prevails in everything."[97]

The incipient universalism of the mystic philosophers advanced the experience of politics so that a return to the symbolic world and the social order of the archaic polis is not possible. Hellenic self-understanding had reached the threshold of a new era in man's search for his humanity and its order. From the discovery of politics emerges the philosophy of politics.

Notes

1. Aristotle *Politics* 1. 11. 9. 1253a.
2. Eric Voegelin, *Order and History,* vol. 2. *The World of the Polis* (Baton Rouge: Louisiana State University Press, 1957), p. 241.
3. Christian Meier, *Die Entstehung des Politischen bei den Griechen* (Frankfurt: Suhrkamp Verlag, 1980), p. 13.
4. Cf. Volker Sellin, "Politik," in *Geschichtliche Grundbegriffe,* vol. 4, ed. Otto Brunner et al. (Stuttgart: Ernst Klett Verlag, 1978); Dolf Sternberger, *Drei Wurzeln der Politik,* vols. 1 and 2 (Frankfurt: Insel Verlag, 1978).
5. *Herodotus* (London: William Heinemann, Loeb Classical Library Series, 1921), 1:30.

6. Ibid., 3:80.
7. Ibid., 7:102-3.
8. Ibid., p. 104; cf. pp. 133-36.
9. Cf. Peter Weber-Schäfer, *Einführung in die antike politische Theorie* (Darmstadt: Wissenschaftliche Buchgesellschaft, 1976), 1:129-34.
10. *Thucydides* (London: William Heinemann, Loeb Classical Library Series, 1919), 2:40.
11. Wolfgang Schadewaldt, *Die Anfänge der Philosophie bei den Griechen* (Frankfurt: Suhrkamp Verlag, 1978), p. 13.
12. Ibid., pp. 15, 178-80; Bruno Snell, *Die Entdeckung des Geistes* (Hamburg: Claassen Verlag, 1955), p. 404; Bruno Snell, *Leben und Meinungen der Sieben Weisen* (München: Heimeran Verlag, 1952).
13. Wolfgang Schadewaldt, *Der Gott von Delphi und die Humanitätsidee* (Frankfurt: Suhrkamp Verlag, 1975), p. 26; cf. Meier, *Entstehung des Politischen,* pp. 73-76; Martin P. Nilsson, *Geschichte der Griechischen Religion* (München: Beck Verlag, 1967), 1:625-53.
14. Schadewaldt, *Philosophie bei den Griechen,* p. 13.
15. Ibid., p. 181.
16. Wilhelm Hoffmann, "Die Polis bei Homer," in *Zur griechischen Staatskunde,* ed. Fritz Geschnitzer (Darmstadt: Wissenschaftliche Buchgesellschaft, 1969), pp. 123-38; Schadewaldt, *Philosophie bei den Griechen,* pp. 47-82; Peter Spahn, *Mittelschicht und Polisbildung* (Frankfurt: Lang Verlag, 1977), pp. 29-58; Arthur W.H. Adkins, *Moral Values and Political Behaviour in Ancient Greece* (New York: Norton, 1972), pp. 10-21; Voegelin, *Order and History* 2:67-110; Hermann Fränkel, *Dichtung und Philosophie des frühen Griechentums* (München: Beck Verlag, 1962), pp. 83-103; Werner Jaeger, *Paideia* (Berlin: Walter de Gruyter, 1936), 1:38-62.
17. Schadewaldt, *Philosophie bei den Griechen,* pp. 82-112; Atkins, *Moral Values,* pp. 22-35; Hans Diller, "Hesiod und die Anfänge der griechischen Philosophie," in *Hesiod,* ed. Ernst Heitsch (Darmstadt: Wissenschaftliche Buchgesellschaft, 1966), pp. 688-707; Fränkel, *Dichtung und Philosophie,* pp. 124-46; Voegelin, *Order and History* 2:126-64; Snell, *Entdeckung des Geistes,* pp. 65-82; Jaeger, *Paideia* 1:89-112.
18. Meier, *Entstehung des Politischen,* pp. 57-70; Chester G. Starr, *The Economic and Social Growth of Early Greece* (New York: Oxford University Press, 1977), pp. 21-46, passim; Spahn, *Mittelschicht,* pp. 59-70; Victor Ehrenberg, *Polis und Imperium* (Zürich: Artemis, 1965), pp. 81-97, 105-38; Victor Ehrenberg, *The Greek State* (London: Methuen, 1969), pp. 3-25; Dieter Nörr, "Vom Griechischen Staat," *Der Staat* 3 (1966): 353-70; W.G. Forrest, *Wege zur Hellenischen Demokratie* (München: Kindler Verlag, 1966).
19. Starr, *Economic and Social Growth,* p. 44.
20. Meier, *Enstehung des Politischen,* pp. 60-63.

21. Konrad H. Kinzl, ed., *Die ältere Tyrannis bis zu den Perserkriegen* (Darmstadt: Wissenschaftliche Buchgesellschaft, 1979).
22. Christian Meier, "Die Identität der Griechen," in *Identität*, ed. Odo Marquard (München: Wilhelm Fink Verlag, 1979), p. 374.
23. Meier, *Entstehung des Politischen*, pp. 71-78; Bernhard Knauss, *Staat und Mensch in Hellas* (Darmstadt: Wissenschaftliche Buchgesellschaft, 1967), pp. 10, 102-5.
24. Schadewaldt, *Philosophie bei den Griechen*, pp. 75-77.
25. Ibid., p. 78.
26. C. Fränkel, *Dichtung und Philosophie*, pp. 147-249; Max Treu, ed., *Archilochos* (München: Heimeran Verlag, 1979); Snell, *Discovery of the Mind*, pp. 42-70; Jaeger, *Paideia* 1:160-86.
27. Meier, *Entstehung des Politischen*, pp. 253-55.
28. Voegelin, *Order and History* 2:120.
29. Meier, *Demokratie*, p. 19.
30. Ibid.
31. Voegelin, *Order and History* 2:195.
32. Ibid., from *Elegy and Iambus* 1, Solon 9-10.
33. *Elegy and Iambus* 1, Solon 4.
34. Ibid., Solon 9-10.
35. Meier, *Demokratie*, p. 19.
36. *Elegy and Iambus* 1, Solon 4.
37. Ibid., Solon 36-37.
38. Ibid., Solon 5.6.
39. Meier, *Demokratie*, p. 20.
40. *Elegy and Iambus* 1, Solon 15.
41. Ibid., Solon 13.
42. Voegelin, *Order and History* 2:197.
43. *Elegy and Iambus* 1, Solon 16.
44. Ibid., Solon 17.
45. Ibid., Solon 34.
46. Meier, *Entstehung des Politischen*, p. 77.
47. Ibid., p. 83.
48. Adkins, *Moral Values*, pp. 37-38.
49. Jaeger, *Paideia* 1:259-71; cf. Fränkel, *Dichtung und Philosophie*.
50. *Elegy and Iambus* 1, Theognis 133-42.
51. Meier, *Entstehung des Politischen*, p. 89.
52. Starr, *Economic and Social Growth*, p. 172.
53. Meier, *Entstehung des Politischen*, p. 289.
54. Spahn, *Mittelschicht*, p. 160.
55. Werner Jaeger, *The Theology of the Early Greek Philosophers* (Oxford: Clarendon, 1947), p. 57.
56. Ibid., p. 58; Nilsson, *Geschichte der Griechischen Religion* 1:708-21.
57. Ibid., p. 721.

58. Voegelin, *Order and History* 2:223-24.
59. Jaeger, *Theology,* pp. 84-85; Snell, *Discovery of the Mind,* pp. 8-17; Nilsson, *Geschichte der Grieschischen Religion* 1:688-703.
60. Walter Burkert, *Grieschische Religion der archaischen und Klassischen Periode* (Stuttgart: Kohlhammer Verlag, 1977).
61. Schadewaldt, *Philosophie bei den Griechen,* p. 269.
62. Jaeger, *Theology,* p. 85.
63. Schadewaldt, *Philosophie bei den Griechen,* p. 270.
64. Jaeger, *Theology,* p. 87.
65. Ehrenbeg, *Polis und Imperium,* p. 279; cf. pp. 253-63.
66. Meier, *Entstehung des Politischen,* p. 284; cf. G. Vlastos, "Isonomia," *American Journal of Philology* 74 (1953): 337-66.
67. Knauss, *Staat und Mensch,* p. 235.
68. Gregory Vlastos, "Isonomia Politike," in *Isonomia,* ed. Jürgen Mau and Ernst G. Schmidt (Berlin: Akademie-Verlag, 1964), p. 9.
69. Meier, *Entstehung des Politischen,* p. 285.
70. Ibid., p. 300.
71. Ibid., p. 302.
72. Schadewaldt, *Philosophie bei den Griechen,* pp. 272, 273, 274; cf. p. 267.
73. Snell, *Discovery of the Mind,* pp. 17, 18.
74. Meier, *Entstehung des Politischen,* pp. 144-246; Eric R. Dodds, *The Ancient Concept of Progress* (Oxford: Clarendon, 1973); Albin Lesky, *Die tragische Dichtung der Hellenen* (Göttingen: Vanden Hoeck u. Rupprecht Verlag, 1972); Hildebrecht Hommel, ed., *Wege zu Aischylos,* 2 vols. (Darmstadt: Wissenschaftliche Buchgesellschaft, 1967); Gregor Sebba, "Die Tragödie," in *Das polische Denken der Griechen,* ed. Peter Weber-Schäfer (München: List Verlag, 1969); Bruno Snell, *Dichtung und Gesellschaft* (Hamburg: Claassen Verlag, 1959); Voegelin, *Order and History* 2:241-66; Jaeger, *Paideia* 1:307-449.
75. *Eumenides* 976.
76. *Agamemnon* 927.
77. Schadewaldt, *Philosophie bei den Griechen,* p. 168; cf. pp. 166-67; Eric Voegelin, "Phronesis," in *Anamnesis* (München: Piper Verlag, 1966).
78. Snell, *Discovery of the Mind,* pp. 184-85.
79. *Eumenides* 517-46.
80. Voegelin, *Order and History* 2:255.
81. Ibid., p. 247.
82. *Suppliants* 407; cf. Snell, *Discovery of the Mind,* pp. 101-3.
83. *Suppliants* 365-69.
84. Ibid., 398.
85. Voegelin, *Order and History* 2:250; *Suppliants* 623-24.
86. Voegelin, *Order and History* 2:263.
87. Schadewaldt, *Philosophie bei den Griechen,* pp. 293-433; Hans-Georg Gadamer, ed., *Um die Begriffswelt der Vorsokratiker* (Darmstadt: Wis-

senschaftliche Buchgesellschaft, 1968); Fränkel, *Dichtung und Philosophie*, pp. 371-88, 398-453; Voegelin, *Order and History* 2:171-80, 184-94, 201-40; Jaeger, *Theology*, pp. 38-54, 90-127; Otto Regenbogen, "Werner Jaeger: die Theologie der frühen griechischen Denker," *Gnomon* 20 (1955).

88. *Elegy and Iambus* 1, Xenophanes 2.
89. Ibid., Xenophanes 23, cf. 1.
90. Herman Diels and Walter Kranz, *Die Fragmente der Vorsokratiker*, vol. 1 (Berlin: Weidmann'sche Buchhandlung, 1956), Parmenides B.1.
91. Schadewaldt, *Philosophie bei den Griechen*, pp. 163-65; Kurt von Fritz, "Die Rolle des Nous," *Begriffswelt der Vorsokratiker*, pp. 246-363; J.R. Warden, "The Mind of Zeus," *Journal of the History of Ideas* 32 (1971): 3-28.
92. Voegelin, *Order and History* 2:209.
93. Diels-Kranz, *Vorsokratiker*, vol. 1, Herakleitos B.116.
94. Ibid., B.2.
95. Ibid., B.89.
96. Ibid., B.73.
97. Ibid., B.114.

Commentary
The Origins of Political Philosophy
VICTOR GOUREVITCH

Professor Gebhardt's paper touches on a wide range of subjects and raises a number of interesting issues. I must, however,
restrict my comments to what I take to be his main argument:
that in sixth- and fifth-century Greece "the political" emerged
and was discovered; that the Greeks' experience of "the political"—of the public life of citizenship and of its place in the
economy of human life as such—is the source and origin of
philosophy in general and political philosophy in particular;
that this Greek understanding of the political as articulated and
transmitted by classical political philosophy remains at least
vestigially alive in our own understanding of political life; that
we should recover and restore this understanding as fully as
possible, for it is "the necessary corrective for the current common opinion that tends to reduce politics to an opaque flux
of power relations in the public domain."

Now this argument seems to me problematic: The attempt
to restore classical political philosophy presupposes that classical
political philosophy continues to be pertinent; and at the least
presupposes that it is independent of the circumstances under
which it arose. Professor Gebhardt evidently holds that it is
so, but only in a comparatively weak sense: Classical political
philosophy has become part and parcel of the West's self-understanding and so has indirectly become an integral part of the
self-understanding of the whole of mankind. Even assuming
this to be the case, it would, of course, not endow classical
political philosophy with any greater rational authority—that
is to say, with any greater pertinence in the only sense that finally
matters—than if it were nothing more than a reflection of an
exclusively Greek experience. It could be said to be pertinent

in the strong sense only if (1) one accepted the Hegelian view that history is the history of a necessary rational development or progress; or (2) the teachings of classical political philosophy were seen as, at a minimum, based on comprehensive reflections about the political and indeed the human alternatives as such. The Hegelian alternative would create more difficulties than it would resolve, and Professor Gebhardt evidently rejects it. He also rejects the second alternative, however. For he denies—or to put it somewhat more cautiously, he appears to deny—the distinction the classics draw between what they regard as the domain of philosophy proper, or theory, and the domain of politics, or practice; and together with this distinction, he denies the primacy or autonomy the classics attribute to theory. In other words, he would appear to deny the foundations of classical political philosophy. It is difficult to be certain whether he really does so because it is difficult to know precisely what he means. In a passage the importance of which he himself underscores—he introduces it by saying "to put my argument most pointedly"—he asserts: "Mankind explicates its humanity in the course of history and, thus, this permanent step in the symbolic self-explication of mankind's humanity, philosophy, originated in politics." One sentence below he adds: " . . . political philosophy [is] the discursive presentation of rational (noetic) acts, acts of thought concerning the order of man in society and history."

Is, then, the primary difference between philosophy and political philosophy that the first consists in "the self-explication of mankind's humanity" and the second in thoughts "concerning the order of man in society and history"? What difference is there between the two? Or does the difference between them consist in that the first is "symbolic," whereas the second is "acts of thought"? What possible evidence could be given in support of such a claim? Is, then, no difference between them? And how are we to understand the claim that Greek philosophy "originated in politics"; or, as he puts it at the conclusion of his summary of some philological studies of early uses of *sophia* and *theoria:* "The evidence is . . . strong that *sophia* and *theoria,* the central tenets of the symbolic form of Hellenic *philos-*

ophia, are grounded in the experiential world of the *présence civique,* the new order of the citizen-polis." What is the force of "originated" and of "grounded in" in such passages? They may merely be intended to remind us that *sophia* and *theoria* had a pre- or nonphilosophical sense and that this is a fact about political life which political philosophy must take into account. But everything in Professor Gebhardt's paper suggests that he means something quite different, that in his view the classical philosophical understanding of theory is dependent on—is a reflection of and not just a reflection about—Greek political life. Everything in his paper suggests that it is to be read as an illustration and a confirmation of the dictum "philosophy is its times grasped in thought."

Plato and Aristotle, on the other hand, agree with each other and with the evidence that philosophy arose independently of Greek political life and prior to political philosophy; that, indeed, Socrates was the first to bring philosophy back to earth. Professor Gebhardt gives no reason why he seeks to rewrite that history. He seems not to have considered sufficiently seriously the possibility that that history may be integral to the classical political philosophers' understanding of their enterprise, that it may therefore be integral to classical political philosophy, and that to reject that history without adequate arguments might therefore be tantamount to blocking the very possibility of understanding classical political philosophy, of recovering it, and *a fortiori* of restoring it even if only sufficiently to serve as "the necessary corrective for the current common opinion" regarding political life.

FREDERICK M. BARNARD

Actions, Reasons, and Political Ideology   2

What is causally most effective or significant in any sequence of occurrences is nearly always a contentious issue. For the purpose of this essay, however, the vital point is not the range or weighing of effective causes in human affairs generally but the possibility of viewing "reasons" as explanatory or justificatory answers in response to "why" questions about *actions*. The principal task, therefore, is to inquire if the conceptual status of action is such as to make the causal relevance of reasons feasible. Likewise, if reasons for actions are to be thought of as "answers," the raising of questions, or at any rate the possibility of questions being raised, seems a plainly crucial requirement. Making sense of actions, in other words, presupposes the asking of questions. In contrast to a traditionalism of acceptance without questioning, a tradition of questioning demands the reopening of questions and the reiteration of justifying answers. Presumably it is in accord with a tradition of questioning that the youngest child capable of posing questions is *expected* to ask questions during the Passover meal—celebrating Israel's exodus from Egypt—so that reasons might be given. Much the same could be said of Plato's dialogues. A story is told because there is something to be learned from the telling. But the telling derives its point or meaning from being itself conceived as a response to the quest for knowing. Similarly, Rousseau wants the general will to be questioned, and not simply upheld, so that it could reply and thereby disclose why it ought to be upheld. Not surprisingly, reasons are more likely to be sought or demanded the less obvious, familiar, or habitual actions are or appear to be. This is, perhaps, why the tracing of *arche* (in its Aristotelian understanding) or of *founding* (in Heidegger's sense) is held to be so exemplary a case of accounting for actions in politics.

The possibility of reasons accounting for actions presupposes, however, in the first place, that reasons *are* capable of providing intelligible answers. And whether they are, clearly hinges on the relation between actions and reasons being other than purely accidental; in which, that is, reasons are not seen as structurally distinct from, but as constitutive of, what is said or done. Unless, therefore, the mediating role of reasons in human action can be shown to be causal in this structural-conceptual sense, there seems little point (I shall argue) in speaking of reasoned political action or a politics of principles and beliefs or ideological politics in any form, pejoratively or non-pejoratively.

I

Giving reasons in politics is understandably associated in our day with the norms and practices of democracies in which public accountability constitutes a defining quality. But that the practice of giving reasons exists at all surely presupposes a cultural context in which men are held generally capable and desirous of asking questions and understanding reasons, at least some of the time. It presupposes also that at least some things are done for reasons and that therefore their authors are in a position to account for what they said or did in terms of reasons. Frequently these presuppositions are linked, if not indeed identified, with the belief in man's capacity for self-direction. And politically, democracy is seen as both the recognition of this capacity and the necessary condition for its effective expression.

The close interlinking of the idea of man's essential autonomy with his capacity for acting on and being moved by reasons, and both these ideas, in turn, with political democracy, is not, however, beyond dispute. Acting on reasons is not a sufficient warrant for autonomous action, and the giving of reasons is not in itself sufficient evidence for the existence of democratic regimes. Ever since the European Enlightenment—whose legacy these linkages for the most part are — doubt has supplanted certainty. Even those who have not taken issue with the underlying assumption, with the idea of man having come of age, or have in fact endorsed it, were far from certain about its implications, particularly its political implications. Rousseau's attempt is undoubtedly the most ingenious ever made to demonstrate the necessary (moral) identity between man's individual autonomy and his political status as a citizen, although even he appears to have been less than sanguine about its actual attainment. Kant, one of his most outstanding admirers, was equally unable to conceal his doubts. In his essay "What Is Enlightenment?" the realization of man having attained *Mündigkeit* — the meaning of which is somewhat lost in translation, since it signifies the capacity to speak for oneself as well as the reaching of adulthood — by no means signals the end to social and political tutelage. Far too large a proportion of men, Kant felt, sadly lack the resolve and courage to make public use of their *Mündigkeit;* and this being so makes it "all too easy for others to set themselves up as their guardians."[1] A revolution, though it might conceivably put an end to autocracy, need not bring about "a true reform of ways of thinking," for new prejudices, like the old ones they replaced, could well serve "as a leash to control the great unthinking mass."[2]

Kant's fears are precisely echoed in Tocqueville's worries over democracy. Just because democracy provides "some of the external forms of freedom," this does not mean that the danger of tutelage or paternalism had passed. The opposite might be nearer the truth. While under the despotic regime of an emperor men would generally be aware of their servitude, they would not necessarily notice the far milder form of paternalism in a democracy. Even if they did, they probably would not mind their will being constantly "softened, bent, and guided." Not tormenting them, democratic paternalism would nevertheless degrade men all the more.[3]

The causal links, then, between acting, the giving of reasons, autonomy, democracy, and the demise of paternalism would appear to be less direct or more tenuous than thinkers of the Enlightenment liked to believe. But whether or not their faith in man's power of, or desire for, self-direction or self-determination was misplaced, the root idea that inspired their faith, the idea that men, in acting upon reasons, are capable of understanding reasons is basic to the practice of giving reasons; it would make no sense at all otherwise. Giving or demanding reasons, therefore, seems feasible only if men understand themselves as agents capable of knowing what they wish to bring about. This self-understanding, though it is a minimal requirement for reasons being given or demanded, is, however, inadequate by itself for conferring meaning upon what is done or is to be done. What is necessary as well is to understand that acting, as a rule, occurs not in isolation of others but with or among others. To be intelligible, therefore, it presupposes some commonality of meaning: What makes sense to me is to make sense to others also. It presupposes further some awareness of the scope and the constraints that arise from the existence of others. Political action, above all, entails a context of others and hence calls for an understanding of this entailment, for a realization, that is, that to act in the political realm is to insert oneself into a particular context of meanings, of opportunities and obstacles, of possibilities and limits.

The way men understand themselves and the way they understand what it is to act among others lend point, then, to the giving or demanding of reasons. These understandings, to be sure, are not constants since they are an integral part of changing cultural contexts. I have no quarrel, therefore, with those who locate man's self-understanding and the way he sees the world around him within the broader stream of "culture" and "tradition." But I hold that it is through these interrelated modes of understanding that "culture" and "tradition" themselves acquire their specific meaning and import at any given time. For whatever continuity exists amid the flux of change does so in and through persisting modes of human understandings, of what Kant called "ways of thinking," Tocqueville meant by "social mores," and Heidegger possibly expressed by the notion of *"Mitsein"*—man's consciousness of sharing a world with others.[4] Cultures and traditions are what they are, they have the identity they have, *because* of certain continuities of understandings without which it would make little sense to speak not only of culture and tradition but also of change. For change has meaning only amid continuity, amid the persistence of some identity.[5]

Undoubtedly, the status of "giving reasons" is not unaffected by the incidence of mendacity within any particular social or political culture in that it markedly bears on the quality of mutual trust and understanding. Yet the possibility that reasons might be used to mask what is done does not rule out the possibility that reasons could truly account for what men do or aspire to do. There is no ground, in other words, for assuming that because men do not always tell the truth, the distinction between truth and falsehood is lost, and all reasons should be taken for mere rationalizations. What appears more basic, therefore, than the incidence of mendacity is whether or not men view themselves as capable of understanding reasons and whether or not reasons are seen as playing a mediating role in human agency. Clearly, if men were not capable of understanding reasons, the giving of reasons would scarcely form a constitutive requirement of a social or political culture. Similarly, if what men say or do had nothing whatsoever in common with the reasons they give, not necessarily because they are lying but because they see no link or only the most tenuous link between reasons and actions, accounting for actions in terms of reasons would be rendered totally otiose. Under such circumstances "ideology" would surely cease to have *any* bearing on political action; there would simply be no use for it.

The burden of argument rests, therefore, on disclosing in what sense, if any, the causality of reasons *in* action constitutes an integral requirement for the possibility of rationally accounting *for* action. In the sections to follow I wish to focus, accordingly, on two interrelated questions or conditions that strike me to be of decisive relevance for the very possibility of speaking of human action in the way we usually do, as a deed carrying meaning for its author. The first inevitably poses the problem of identifying a particular deed with a particular author, which clearly hinges on the ability and willingness of man to

choose a course of action for reasons he is prepared to acknowledge as his own. The second question concerns the possibility
of reasons having causal power or, at any rate, causal relevance
in regard to action. Directly or indirectly, answers to these questions might clarify the role of ideology in politics as they might
help determine whether or not political ideologies could be
viewed in terms other than those of deception or false consciousness.

II

In attributing a deed to a person we usually ask how free he
was in bringing it about. And when we think of freedom in
this context, we generally think about it in the way that Hobbes
did, as having essentially two faces: one glancing backward to
antecedent conditions, the other looking ahead to what is to
be accomplished. We have become accustomed to distinguishing
between these two faces of freedom in terms of negative and
positive freedom; a practice not without merit but at the same
time liable to mislead in that it tends to confuse a half-truth
with the whole truth. I prefer to simply follow Hobbes, for
whom both faces appear to be like two sides of a single coin
or, to change metaphors once more, two dimensions of one
and the same thing. One is the absence of external impediments,
the other the use of man's internal power of reason and judgment "to do what he would."[6] It is the second, or internal, dimension of freedom, the doing of what one would, that is the
major concern of this section. Only if men at least some of
the time wish to do "their own thing" is there a sense in conferring upon events the status of action.

Whether opportunities for acting (in this sense) exist is
clearly a question inseparably connected with the environment
in which men find themselves, for it provides the space as it
also structures the range and distinctive style of action. Human
agency, therefore, is a status that, in requiring a context, is at
the same time exposed to its hazards and oportunities. All the
same, the external conditions that hinder or promote man's in-
sertion into his environment do not in themselves constitute
sufficient conditions for the occurrence of action, for they say

nothing about man's internal source of acting. Wherein lies this source? This question was of course one of the principal considerations Rousseau addressed in his political philosophy and Kant in his moral philosophy. And insofar as they both give prominence to man's capacity for understanding reasons and his ability to act upon them, their conception of human autonomy tells us something important about the internal sources of human action. Directly or indirectly, it touches on three core ideas of paramount relevance for our purpose: (1) the idea that a person is capable of understanding himself as an agent who can say or do things for reasons of his own; (2) the idea that a person is capable of recognizing purposes and of choosing between them; and (3) the idea that existential givens, though they delimit a person's control or mastery over events, do not render him incapable of understanding himself as a self-directing agent.

As a matter of common experience, men find it difficult to "own up" when they cannot appropriate the reasons for which a thing was done as their own reasons. Under these circumstances, the only "reasons" they might give would refer to psychological or physical states of one sort or another *from* which they presumably acted the way they did; but these would not be reasons *for* which they acted. In the absence of such reasons, what allegedly was done came about inadvertently, because of physical or emotional stress, blind rage, or the influence of drugs. The essential basis, then, for our ability to account for what we did is the possession of some knowledge of what we purposively were trying to achieve rather than the existence of antecedent psychophysical states that "made us do" what we allegedly did. This minimal awareness of purposive direction sets apart action from mere doing.

"Knowledge" also normally includes some awareness of the context in which we act, some recognition of the opportunities or obstacles that confront us. Above all it involves awareness of a space inhabited by others. Ends or purposes are not chosen within a contextual vacuum; unless we think of human actions as the deeds of solitary men, enacted under some "veil of ignorance," or as though they were miracles surfacing from the unknown, like meteors dropping out of skies,[7] we have to view them against a background of institutional structures, systems of rules, roles, and mutual understandings, and to concede that purposive choice is not unlimited or unbounded. Purposes, in other words, are chosen from within alternatives that for the most part are givens; not givens fixed once and for all, but givens all the same at the point of choosing. The function of any social arrangement that qualifies as an "order" is to offer some guidance as to what can be achieved by pursuing certain ends and what obstacles may have to be faced in so doing. In short, a social order is an order because it provides through its structures and rules a recognizable space for purposive action.

This is not to say that social orders and their institutional structures *determine* human purposes. No such causality is intended in my directing attention to the location or context of purposive choice. Contexts are not causes; though grounded for the most part in existential givens, human purposes are not derivative from them as an oak is from an acorn. External limiting conditions, moreover, whether perceived or not, merely govern the range of choice; they do not by themselves characterize choice in itself. Knowledge of external conditions certainly makes for informed action; it enables us to choose with at least some awareness of the opportunities or obstacles facing us. But to discover that choice *itself* is inherently limited is to know what it is to act; it is to realize that being free to act *consists* in choosing within ineradicable limitations. Absolute choice, like absolute freedom, is an absurdity. Freedom, particularly political freedom, to assume meaning requires perimeters or boundaries; limitless freedom, freedom devoid of the need for choosing between alternatives, gives us no ground for acting one way or another.

An understanding of ourselves as self-directing agents must therefore be tempered by a recognition of the limits within which human freedom is bounded. "Autonomy," if it is to have any meaning for action — particularly political action — can imply neither absolute mastery nor absolute independence: to control anything at will or to make one's way in the world unaided.

No man made himself entirely by himself.[8] To make individual autonomy contingent on the complete absence of limits, influences, or interferences is to lose sight of what it is to be human. To confine so rigorously the meaning of autonomy, moreover, so broadens the connotation of "manipulation" as to render it, too, virtually meaningless.[9]

Clearly, to describe *all* external influences in terms of manipulation is to deprive it of whatever distinctive meaning it has. Usually we apply the term to influences or interferences we resent, not to those we accept or even welcome. We would hardly deny, for example, that our manners, attitudes, tastes, or prejudices are sizably the work of some external agents or that language itself, though we may rarely be aware of it, is in fact external to us. For while our usage is scarcely independent of language, language exists independently of our usage. Anyone who had to switch to a new language will have noticed that it continuously controls and patterns our thoughts, that, in other words, it not merely expresses them but decisively shapes or molds them.[10] We do not, however, speak of such molding as manipulation since, as a rule, we do not view it as the deliberate design of particular individuals or groups or as being at odds with ourselves. That we do not do so suggests that we generally perceive a difference between acceptable and unacceptable interference and between what is and what is not incongruent with where *we* want to go. Unless, therefore, we have no option but to assume men to be wholly plastic, and wholly plastic in completely identical ways—so that external influences not only mold them but mold them uniformly—we need not conclude that human action is bereft of autonomy and individuality of any sort.[11] All we need to concede is that whatever forms or areas of self-direction exist do so not in the absence but in spite of limits, obstacles, and interferences and that, therefore, "autonomy" implies some sort of continuously shifting balance, or tension, between the existential given and the aspired nongiven of human agency.

Modern man, though he is emboldened to think that he can master his environment, is at the same time constantly made aware of the limits to his mastery. It is this bipolar tension between "mastery" and "subjection" that struck Rousseau and Kant so forcibly. Kant attributed it to the effect that the advances of natural science have on man's self-understanding. For the same science that feeds his pride and inspires his confidence in controlling the world around him also undermines his consciousness of freedom. It goads him into flying as it clips his wings, treating him, the master, as a mere product of natural processes over which he has but little control.[12]

Thus, while a sense of mastery over nature provides some empirical ground for man's understanding of himself as an autonomous agent, it by no means characterizes that understanding itself. In the final analysis, human autonomy appears to require a form of "verification" that is inherently different from empirical proof or evidence in the customary "factual" sense, for it entirely hinges on an internal or conceptual—and thus nondemonstrable—capacity for realizing the area in which we *can* knowingly choose and act. Reasons, as purposive or directional grounds for action, can accordingly have causal efficacy only if they are understood, believed in, or accepted. They do not do their job in the manner a knife cuts bread. Since reasons, thus conceived, are at best mediate causes, their causality presents us with problems that we are spared in causal inquiries into mechanical operations or natural processes. And perhaps it is, above all, in virtue of this "structural" difference that rational causality so emphatically defies being treated as though it were a simple analogue of causality in its generally accepted "scientific" sense.

III

Since I have now several times invoked the concept of rationality, I had better clarify the way in which I invoke it. From what has so far been said about the "rational" structure of action it should be evident that I am not concerned with what Max Weber called *Wertrationalität,* that is, a substantive value or end with which rationality could be identified. Nor am I concerned with the more commonly applied meaning of rationality as instrumental rationality, with what Weber called *Zweckrationalität,* according to which rationality consists in using the most effective means toward the promotion of given ends or interests. Least of all do I wish to merge or blend formal and substantive understandings of rationality in the manner John Rawls appears to be doing in his *A Theory of Justice.* Instead, for the purpose of this discussion, I want to leave aside the question of substantive content that the concept of rationality so worryingly begs. Thus, while I agree with Rawls (and Hart) that rationality implies intentionality, that is, having a reason for acting, I do not maintain that having a reason for acting is tantamount to having a good reason (in *any* objective sense of good) or having truth or justice on one's side. For, in contrast to substantive "rationalists," I invoke a more limited conception of rationality, viewing it purely as a *modality,* as the form or manner in which positions are assumed or justified. Beliefs, including political ideologies, have on this view a rational foundation if they are defensible or challengeable, if reasons in their support can be offered or demanded. Thus understood, rationality serves as a presupposition of contestability: Giving reasons make contestation *possible.* I do concede that rationality in this sense can serve this function only if reasons given contain *some* shared elements of meaning. To be intelligible (though not necessarily acceptable) to others, reasons cannot be wholly private whims. It is precisely because private whims do not lend themselves to rational explanation (in that no intelligible reasons can be offered) that they are not open to rational contestation either. Openness to contestation, moreover, via rationality as a modality, guards against first-person accounting unduly succumbing to the temptation of utter solipsism.

We agreed earlier that men can render account only for what they choose to do and not for what "makes them do" what they do; that existential givens constitute the context, if not also in large measure the perimeters of what they can and cannot "reasonably" do. But in admitting all this we merely recognize the obvious: that there are boundaries to our rationality *in* choosing, whatever may be said about the rationality *of* choosing. Recognizing this, we simply realize that it may not always be easy to distinguish with certainty antecedent existential conditions (our "reasons *from*") from genuine purposes or directional guides (our "reasons *for*"); but we do not thereby deny the validity of the distinction as such. Putting it differently, in recognizing the causal influence of existential givens we certainly limit the range of rational causality, but we do not thereby rule it out. The question of rational causality would then essentially come to this: If reasons do not necessarily account for actions—in that they may fail to explain them or to explain them adequately enough—in what sense, if any, do they bear upon actions? A short answer could be something like this: Unless reasons were contained, so to speak, in what we do, what we do could not even *count* as "action." Although I believe this answer to touch the heart of the matter, the notion of "having reasons" possibly calls for some elaboration.

Two things, above all, need further spelling out. First, "having reasons" need not exclude the possibility that reasons offered as explanations or justifications of an action are not the same as those that in fact founded or grounded it. In an age or culture in which the giving of reasons is expected if not demanded, the tendency to invent post hoc reasons, not necessarily to deceive but simply out of embarrassment for having forgotten the original reasons or being reluctant to reveal them, may indeed be widespread. But not unless such rationalizations assume proportions that render reasons indistinguishable from lies would the giving of reasons, no less than the asking for reasons, become utterly pointless. Second, the fact of having reasons as grounds for acting does not necessarily constitute a sufficient condition for action to occur since "having reasons" does not imply a commitment to act. Action-promoting reasons do not operate like mechanical causes. We are not compelled to leave a political party simply because we might have good reasons for so doing, having, for example, found out about the lying, the corruption, the terror, and so on, practiced by its leading functionaries. For just as we may act blindly by not knowing what we are doing, we may turn a blind eye to what we know. [13] *Having* reasons, in other words, is not the same as minding reasons. Yet even when we do mind reasons, we may fail to act on them, either because we are aware of some strong counter-reasons or because we do not feel courageous (or ruthless, disloyal, or disgusted) enough. We can never blandly assume, therefore, that our perception of reality, and the beliefs we form in the light of our perception, have direct causal power in regard to our propensity to act. Thus, recognizing wrongdoing in the party or unfair distribution of rewards in the economy need not turn us into agitators, reformers, or revolutionaries. There simply is no inexorable causal continuity between perception, reasons, and commitments to action. Since acting usually involves choice, and choice frequently means deciding between such opposing reasons (or rules) as telling the truth to the secret police and saving innocent people seeking refuge, having or minding *a* reason that one could act upon may indeed be a most complicated business that, because of its complexity, may result in inaction, not by design—in which case it is clearly a form of action—but simply by default, through persistent procrastination or agonizing indecisiveness.

But if having reasons for acting is not causal knowledge, should one conclude that reasons have no causal power whatsoever? Certainly, if having reasons would invariably fail to move men to act, we could not conclude otherwise. In point of fact, the position is less straightforward and a good deal more puzzling. For do we not find reasons wholly ineffective at one point in time (or with one person) and powerfully decisive at another point in time (or with another person)? Yet, puzzling though it may seem, we know from experience that no contradiction is necessarily involved; that, to be considered absurd or abnormal, such occurrences are too much of a commonplace. We are forced to wonder, therefore, whether a large part of our perplexity over the lack of rational causality or the fickleness of it should not be attributed to our tendency of drawing the connection between knowing and acting, or between having reasons and being moved by them to act, too tightly. Some philosophers, raising this question, have thought it best to abandon the notion of rational causality altogether.[14] I am reluctant to follow this line of thought; I am as unwilling, that is, to make the separation between action-guiding reasons and action too severe as I am unwilling to draw the connection too close. For I simply cannot see what sense it makes to speak of something as a reason for acting if it has absolutely no capacity for influencing choice. Decisions, based on reasons, evidently *do* cause actions. It would seem therefore that to say that reasons do not operate like mechanical causes is not to commit oneself to a denial of causality *tout court*. Clearly, there are dis-analogies; for one thing, mechanical causes to be causes must invariably show the same concomitant effects; for another, mechanical causes cannot be assessed as good or bad. At the same time, there are analogies too. Surely, what makes an utterance a *reason* is its explanatory or justificatory propensity, which it would not have if men were never to act upon reasons. Yet to affirm the possibility of reasons being viewed as causes is not to imply that rational causality is inextricably tied to the notion of so-called law-governed uniformities. In other words, to find a reason to have been the necessary condition of an action is not the same as to claim that such an action must inevitably ensue whenever an identical reason is being held. Likewise, having been moved by reasons to do what one did by no means implies that one could not have acted differently. To state, therefore, that an action has been caused is not to maintain that it was inevitable.

All the same, the notion of "acting on reasons" does imply the recognition of intentionality and purposiveness, and the practice of "giving reasons" does imply their potential use as explanations or justifications. In turn, intentionality and purposiveness imply that whatever was done for whatever reasons carried a meaning for the actor. This inherent meaning cannot be disclosed analogously to the uncovering of psychophysical or sociological causes. For what the latter would reveal would be of an altogether different order from what an agent sees in what he does as a self-acknowledged author of an action. It would explain only what the agent himself cannot rationally account for, what he fails to recognize as *his* reasons for acting; and, in so doing, it would explain only that which is devoid of meaning for the agent himself. He may still be held responsible for what he "did," but he cannot be expected to appropriate what he has done as his own *action* if he can see no point in having done it.[15]

48

It follows that what principally matters is that reasons are entailed, or at any rate are seen as entailed, in what we say or do in order to *account* for our actions. But whether they are viewed as entailments or not will depend on the sense they make, the meaning they yield, to the actor himself or to those asking for reasons to be given. Reasons-as-entailments, therefore, are not causal antecedents in the customary sense but logical properties that actions, in order to count as *actions,* must possess. Whether reasons were "there" is, accordingly, a question not of physical fact but of conceptual understanding. Clearly, if reasons appear unconnected with what was done, or only most tenuously connected, they will be ignored or at best considered suspect and hence be of little *practical* interest. In that event, accounting for an "action" may indeed by primarily, if not entirely, a matter of investigating glands, hormones, reflexes, income tax returns, climate, or pollution counts.

IV

I attempt now to relate what so far has been said about actions, reasons, rationality, and rational causality to the status and function of political ideology. Three salient points should be noted by way of summing up the argument until now, for they form the principal assumptions of what is to follow. I identified as "action" what men do whenever they act upon reasons of their own choosing. Action, thus understood, is accordingly characterized by autonomous choice and the immanence of reasons. Because of the internal merging of action and reasons, I spoke of a "rational structure" of action, by virtue of which actions are explicable, discussable, and contestable. Second, I identified "rationality" as a modality, as the form or manner in which positions are assumed and justified or beliefs held and defended. Third, I identified "rational causality" as the effective mediation of reasons in action. While I granted that reasons do not operate like mechanical causes, I did not rule out rational causality *tout court;* and while I recognized that the causal efficacy of reasons need not contain their validity or, conversely, that valid reasons need not contain causal efficacy, I nonetheless maintained that the notion of "reason" does imply its potential use as a causal explanation or purposive justification and that the use of rationalizations as explanations and justifications does not exclude the possibility of professed reasons being true reasons.

The conclusion of the previous secton and the general tenor of my argument so far leave little doubt that I consider explorations into nonrational sources of human behavior to be of a different order and function from explorations into rational causes. Whereas the former may supply explanations that we seek in vain by examining professed reasons, explorations of rational causes are capable of disclosing meanings that we could not expect to discover by the methods of psychology, sociology, or the medical sciences. Certainly, if our purpose is to uncover the *origins* of beliefs (or ideologies), we might do well to study the social structure, economic background, psychic needs, and so on, of those holding them. But to uncover such socioeconomic or psychophysical "causes" would scarcely disclose what men did for what reasons or purposes or reveal whatever point they saw in what they aspired. For reasons (and meanings) possess a cognitive status of their own independently of their nonrational genesis. Similarly, we have to think of the causal efficacy of reasons as something independent of their nonrational source. The principal concern of this section, therefore, is to inquire into the possibility of viewing ideology as a form of "consciousness," the rational structure of which could be said to have both cognitive independence and causal efficacy. The approach will be by way of making a distinction between reasons as beliefs and reasons as commitments.

Beliefs could of course be mistaken, and mistaken beliefs could of course assume the form of self-deception. I would hesitate, however, to go so far as Hannah Arendt has done in speaking of self-deception as "lying to oneself."[16] I may refuse to abandon beliefs I come to recognize as false (out of loyalty, opportunism, or sheer stubborness), but if I know them to be false, I am not lying to myself, I am simply lying. On the other hand, if indeed I do believe what is plainly wrong (out of ignorance, superstition, or inflexibility of thinking), I may well be deceived, but I am not lying, neither to myself nor to anyone

else, for lying obviously implies a deliberate effort to deceive.
As I argued elsewhere, one can have false beliefs but one cannot believe falsely.[17] Whereas beliefs are propositions that can
be true or false, believing is an activity or a state of mind that
exists or does not exist but that cannot be true or false. Being
enveloped in fog or manipulated by means of fabricated smoke-
screens will undoubtedly blur my vision in the manner drugs
may change my perception; whatever I see, think, or do would
spring from such sources of self-deception, and in this sense
I would certainly be acting from a false consciousness. However, "false consciousness" in the way in which Marx and Engels applied it to "ideology" (in the *German Ideology*) entails
not merely cognitive implications but also moral implications—
seeing things distorted as opposed to wilfully distorting things.
And while it may have served their polemical purposes not to
distingush too insistently between delusions and deceptions,
nothing but confusion ensues from conflating deceiving with
being deceived. But whether our beliefs are mistaken or not,
they do not in themselves constitute commitments to action.
We found earlier that there is no unbroken continuity between
holding certain beliefs—or having reasons for acting—and acting upon them. What is it, then, that constitutes the gap between having reasons and acting upon them, between, say, holding something to be unjust and expressing this belief in some
form of protest? More to the point, what transfoms such reasons
as beliefs into reasons as commitments?

I wish to suggest that the distinction between reasons as
beliefs and reasons as commitments is a *radical* distinction.
What is involved is not a change in degree but a change in kind;
I see this switch in terms of what I might call a "conversion,"
a sort of metamorphosis of consciousness, and I regard it as
"radical" because it cannot simply be equated with a sharpened
form of perception, with, say, a more intense awareness of injustice, as in our example. One does not suddenly see what
one did not see before, in the manner a biologist discovers new
data under the microscope. In a certain sense, therefore, it is
not a strictly cognitive change at all. One merely sees *for oneself*
something one has known all along. Somewhat as in Plato's

Meno, one recovers a meaning that was there for the grasping. In short: We do not know more, we know *differently.* Unlike logical inferences, a sense of commitment cannot be deduced. In the final analysis, it is an act of personal discovery as mysterious as it is potentially heroic, fanatical, redemptive, or destructive.

I am unable to generalize about the conditions or circumstances apt to bring about this change, whether they essentially consist in external molding, if not manipulation, or in an internal conversion of experience comparable to that of St. Paul. But I doubt if there is a specific property in reasons themselves that qualifies them either as reasons qua beliefs or as reasons qua commitments. Nor can I—rather regretfully—see what difference it makes to the switch from mere belief to actual commitment if it results from authentic information and experience rather than from people being deliberately fed with lies; for the causal efficacy of the switch seems wholly independent of the nature of its genesis. A sense of commitment, to be sure, seems inseparable from a sense of conviction; and to be convinced of a reason one has to believe it to be true. Still, the conviction of having truth (or justice) on one's side in itself tells us nothing about the manner in which it is held; whether or not, that is, reasons are or could be given in its support. Similarly, a conviction, and the intensity with which it is cherished, constitutes no sufficient warrant for its capacity of being translated into political action. Although it may not be possible to state in positive terms what might determine an ideology's action-promoting, if not action-compelling propensity, it is surely doubtful whether the degree of conviction with which it is held is a causally decisive indicator. For espousing ideologies in politics and acting upon them involves not merely—if I may rather improperly borrow here from theology—"faith" but also "works." Whatever merit they might have as "belief systems" could be more than offset by their lack of appeal or credibility as guides to political action. But if a total dedication to "faith" could thus prove politically disastrous, a total dedication to "works" could mean the end of ideology itself. For a completely pragmatic ad hoc style of politics, if it were at all conceivable, would have no need of ideology of any sort. It follows that an ideological style of politics—about which more is to be said in the following section—is viable only if convictions or principled positions contain at least a potential for their translation into action.

We may then tentatively conclude that, while the rational structure of "political ideology" consists in its capacity for articulating intelligibly coherent grounds for political action, its causal status hinges on its capacity for serving as a credible guide for the practical attainment of political ends. Putting it differently, for a political ideology to possess rationality *as well as* causal efficacy it must contain reasons qua beliefs that at least potentially are convertible into reasons qua commitments.

V

Since political action, particularly in democratic contexts (in the broadest and most varied sense), is not confined to deeds attributable to single individuals—"great men" or hereditary notables—but comprises different kinds and degrees of joint or collective undertakings, the question arises of how it is possible for men to act in concert with others and yet acknowledge the reasons given for such undertakings as their own reasons. In essence this is of course the same question Rousseau set himself to resolve in his *Social Contract*. Clearly, any attempt that seeks to view political action as a species of human action—involving intentionality and accountability—must regard this question as its most paramount concern.

I wish to suggest that what makes possible the assumption of an analogy between the rational structure of political action and the rational structure of personal action, or of "action" as it is ordinarily understood, is the mediation of political ideology. For I see in this mediation a means whereby political action may be identifiable with recognizable agents capable of acting for reasons that they regard as their own reasons. This presupposes of course that within the limitations of time and place men are playwrights as well as players.

The extent to which collective purposes can ever be made to wholly coincide with individual purposes is not solely a matter of writing the right plot or finding the right organizational means. But insofar as joint purposes and collective problems are amenable to conceptual and organizational solutions, which are not merely bureaucratically imposed but associatively generated, the mediation of some common understandings will be required whereby a group of men could act jointly and yet feel severally accountable for what is done. The point to note here is that a group does not see itself as something *distinct* from shared understandings but as *constitutive* of them. In other words, associative groups are what they are *because* of their shared understandings; they express, rather than create, a shared social or political consciousness. In this section I want to sort out, albeit in the briefest possible way, what kind of properties political ideology needs to possess in order to provide this mediation, to supply, that is, the constitutive ground for the emergence and continuity of political associations or parties.

In the first place, political ideologies should be capable of being viewed as causal rather than merely reductively caused. Notwithstanding that ideologies might be said in some sense to "reflect" social structures, communal values, or economic interests, it is imperative that ideologies could themselves be seen as causal agents in political development and political processes generally. For example, in contrast to looking upon the spread of ideologies from the West as the *result* of the disruption of traditional religious societies, it should not be impossible to view them as capable of having themselves brought about this disruptive change.

Second, although I do not deny that political ideologies borrow from generalizing philosophical *Weltanschauungen,* I wish to suggest that it is not *Weltanschauungen* per se that give rise to ideologies but that ideologies, conceived as guides for and explanations of courses of political action, merely draw on broader belief systems as they serve their organizational and policy needs. For the belief systems have an existence independent from the use to which they are applied, while ideologies come into their own only within specific contexts of organization and argument. The former are, so to speak, the elements of universality from which particular lines of action derive their justifying anchorage or grounding.

What Hume and Tocqueville had to say about political principles may help clarify this point. In his well-known essay "Of the Original Contract" Hume speaks of philosophical or speculative principles as "annexed" to their political or practical use, as a "fabric" reared to "protect and cover that scheme of actions which it (a party) pursues."[18] Hume succeeds well in bringing out the close interlacing of "principles" and "organization," which to me represents the essence of what I call an "ideological style" of politics. The interlacing consists precisely in striking a balance between the need for general justification and the demands of particular application, between "philosophy" and "politics." The philosophically backed reasons for political action could no doubt in effect (if not necessarily in intent) protect or conceal collective interests or purposes, as Hume observes. But it does not follow from this that such "covering" principles are nothing but rationalizations. If Hume is not entirely unequivocal on the use of principles, Tocqueville certainly is. That principles were constantly sacrificed to petty and transitory ambitions and interests was of course no news to Tocqueville; yet he refused to *identify* principles with interests. "Although there is little of the metaphysician in my make-up, I have always been struck by the influence that metaphysical opinions have had on things which appear far removed from them," he writes in a letter.[19] Tocqueville rejected the identification of principles with interests not merely because it would mean the denial of morality in politics but also because it would mean a gross distortion of political reality itself. An ideological style of politics—in the form of principled positions—was for Tocqueville the hallmark of a civilized nation. A wholly pragmatic politics, if he thought it conceivable at all, could be practiced only by "barbarians," for they "are the only society in which politics can be recognized as being confined to practice."[20] In this view, action guided by general precepts and reasoned argument, as opposed to ad hoc improvisation or capricious fiat, hinges on perceiving the concrete and particular through some generalizing or universalizing prism, when "perceive" connotes not merely cognitive awareness but evaluative understanding comparable to what I earlier called "minding." Politics, for

Tocqueville, becomes civilized if and when men have learned to conceptualize their experience and as a result view at least some events as the outcome of human agency prompted by general ends.[21] In turn, general ends, which are no longer wholly "metaphysical," render possible (if not necessary) a mode of practical reasoning that, when applied to the public realm, is quite properly describable as "ideological" in very much the sense in which Hume and Tocqueville speak of the use of philosophical principles.

Third, although an ideological style of public reasoning—thus understood—is not generally characterized by an internal consistency of strict logical rigor, this in itself does not constitute a disabling quality or necessary defect. For what adequately sustains an ideology is not strict intrinsic logic but plausible extrinsic intelligibility. Unless we definitionally equate ideology with rationalization in the manner in which we frequently identify rhetoric with sophistry, there is no ground for dismissing either as mere verbal trickery. Rather, in the light of what has been said so far, ideology may be viewed as a form of reasoning that, approximating roughly Aristotle's concept of the enthymeme, conforms with the requirements of rational discourse in terms of what we earlier called "modal rationality." Putting it slightly differently, we might say that "ideology" could claim a cognitive status of its own along with, yet distinct from, strict syllogistic argument or scientific theory. Soundness in the latter is judged by criteria intrinsic to the methods of philosophical or scientific inquiry, and whatever truths they yield are independent of popular appeal or widely persuasive intelligibility. A political ideology, by contrast, is a form of rational discourse whose cogency, coherence, or indeed "logic," is never wholly detachable from its capacity for rallying support by providing persuasive grounds for concerted action. Perceived or presumed causal relevance for action may thus be said to form an integral component of an ideology's "rationality" or cognitive intelligibility.

Finally, let me turn once more to the question of ideological commitment and the related question of ideological constraint. Clearly, every ideological commitment is a two-sided

affair, encompassing leaders as well as followers. We are generally inclined—possibly under the influence of Robert Michels's
so-called iron law of oligarchy—to attribute considerable discre-
tionary powers to elites. The danger is that this might lead us
to underrate the very real constraints ideologies could impose
on the extent of such powers. Wittgenstein's observation that
"the limits of my language mean the limits of my world" has,
in this connection, its undoubted relevance.[22] For ideologies
could be viewed as conceptual boundaries to our way of thinking about "what is" and about "what is to be done." Publicly
avowed principles, enshrined in a political ideology, can and
do set such boundaries to the scope for doctrinal and organizational change and thereby to the latitude of political processes
in general and the wheeling and dealing of elites in particular.
Unless followers feel pledged to unconditional allegiance—to
"party" or "personalities"—leaders can ill afford to lose public
face by wilfully disregarding ideological constraints.

At the same time, the scope and permanence of ideological
constraints should not be exaggerated. Neither leaders nor followers in any political context are the sole authors or control-
lers of change. There is thus no reason to suppose that changing reality cannot itself generate a need for the reappraisal of
conceptual boundaries and their eventual extension in order
to accommodate it. In other words, ideological conceptualiza-
tions are not immune to change and to men's shared need to
come to terms with change; for a conceptualization of political
reality that ceases to mesh with what is new cannot but call
for rethinking. It follows that experience of reality need not
be thought of as wholly a captive of ideological categories or
political language generally. Should, therefore, custodians of
an ideology wish to manipulate conceptual constraints, they
can never altogether ensure that they, the trappers, do not become ensnared by their own traps.

VI

By way of conclusion, I might add a couple of qualifications
to the two central positions assumed here. I argued, in the first
place, that human agency, to be intelligible in terms of mean-

ingful conduct, demands reasons to be contained in action, and so reasons might quite properly be thought of as structural requirements of the concept of action. From this it could be deduced that I view the relation between action and reasons as a form of unity. I do not wish to deny that such an inference may correctly be drawn; I do, however, want this vision of unity to be emphatically kept apart from conceptions of "unity" which view it as a sort of harmony between theory and practice. For I do not imply that action in any sense confirms or denies the validity of reasons and thereby establishes their truth or falseness. Furthermore, while I insist that conduct to qualify as action has to entail reasons, I do not insist that the reverse holds good, that reasons entail actions. Thus, in postulating a measure or form of unity between action and reasons I imply no necessary reversibility or symmetry and, consequently, no prescriptive demand for matching words with deeds or reasons with actions.

In the second place, I wished to maintain that there is nothing in the nature of a human purpose that precludes its serving as a reason for joint commitments. On this assumption I consider political ideologies capable of mediating the marriage of individual and collective reasons for action. Admittedly, this mediation may in fact prove exceedingly difficult in that it may encounter problems in attempting to resolve conflicts posed by a mix of collective purposes, only some of which one would wish to recognize as one's own. Here the burden lies in deciding in each case whether, on balance, one can sustain one's allegiance to a common cause or ought to opt out—a choice not easily made.[23] Notwithstanding this practical difficulty, joint commitments on the basis of a shared ideology do yield the possibility of conceiving of political action, in terms of both participation and accountability, as a variant of recognizable human agency.

The drift of my argument, however, was not to claim that action in politics was indistinguishable from action in private life. Whether or not we hold that political actions, to rank as great and memorable deeds, need to be unfettered by considerations of private morality, history certainly does not lead us

to expect standards or criteria regnant in one realm to be equally or invariably applicable to the other. *Arche* and *founding*,
though they may unquestionably qualify as great deeds, do not
inevitably escape the risk of "dirty hands"—a lesson Machiavelli
was so determined to get across to us. There is no denying that
this is a seriously disquieting problem bedeviling the relation
between ethics and politics; but it is not a central issue in this
discussion. My principal concern was not whether the nature
of *moral* reasoning in the two realms is intrinsically analogous,
but rather if, and in what sense, accounting for actions is *possible,* and accounting for joint actions *conceivable.* With these
questions in mind, I suggested that, for acting in politics to
be a species of a common genus of action, it had to contain
something that men could recognizably appropriate as their
own. The locus of this recognizable "something" I sought to
identify with reasons, insofar as these form a constitutive part
of action, by virtue of which political life is capable of assuming a quality that we normally associate with purposive conduct in personal life.[24] And in relating this possibility to man's
problematic understanding of himself as an actor and not solely
as a victim, and to his equally worrisome understanding of what
it is to act with others, I merely singled out two conditions without which it seems to make little sense to speak of human agency in either realm—at any rate in the (arguably illusory) way
in which we commonly do.

Given these twofold conditions, action could be viewed
as akin to *praxis,* and whatever measure of understanding or,
more precisely, whatever understanding of measure that it contained, as akin to *sophia,* provided that this is not taken to imply that it is the function of *sophia* to yield practical results
or to solve practical problems. We may indeed be unable to
conceive of *praxis* without *sophia*—since *praxis* wholly bereft
of *sophia* would fail to count as "action"—but we can quite properly speak of *sophia* in the absence of *praxis.* For *sophia,* like
"theory" (in its original meaning), has a cognitive status of its
own, independent of the uses to which it is put. What R. G.
Collingwood once said about theory could therefore be applied
here to *sophia:* Its role is not to solve problems but to clear

them of misunderstandings that make their solution impossible.[25]

It might of course be objected that I am taking liberties with the classical notion of *sophia,* that the way I am pressing it into service comes closer to the meaning of sophistry than to that of *sophia.* Arguably, there is point to this objection; I concede that the use I make of it is a stipulated use. At the same time I believe that in so doing I inflict no undue injury to its root meaning. For what the two modes of understanding singled out in this essay involve is an act of conceptual discovery that differs radically from forms of knowledge that yield answers in mechanical operations or natural processes. And it is typically this unique kind of knowing that is called for when men engage in action, when, that is, what they do has point or meaning for them. Such knowledge, to be sure, rarely if ever attains the full measure of *sophia.* Were it to contain none of its measure, however, to speak in the manner I have done of man's understanding of himself as an agent and of his understanding of the world as a space in which to insert himself, would surely be little short of an absurdity. For what these understandings entail *is,* above all, a sense of *measure,* in and through which *sophia* most profoundly manifests itself in action, and in political action par excellence.[26] There can be little doubt that *arche* or *founding* is unthinkable in the absence of political vision; yet to sustain *founding,* political vision can ill dispense with measure, with that serene awareness which unfailingly grasps that to act politically is to act amid possibilities *and* limits. To say, therefore, that questions are asked so that reasons might be given is in a sense merely a way of redescribing the perpetual search for whatever measure *sophia* may confer upon action or reveal it to possess.

Notes

Work on this essay was done in conjunction with a research project on "Accounting for Actions," assisted by a Research Time Stipend of the Social Sciences and Humanities Research Council of Canada.

Actions, Reasons, and Political Ideology

1. Immanuel Kant, "An Answer to the Question: 'What Is Enlightenment?'" in *Kant's Political Writings,* ed. Hans Reiss (London: Cambridge University Press, 1970), p. 54.

2. Ibid., p. 55.

3. Alexis de Tocqueville, *Democracy in America,* ed. J.P. Mayer (New York: Doubleday, 1969), vol. 2, pt. 4, chap. 6, pp. 691-93.

4. Martin Heidegger, *Vom Wesen des Grundes* (Halle, 1929), trans. Terrence Malick, *The Essence of Reasons,* bilingual ed. (Evanston, Ill.: Northwestern University Press, 1969), p. 100.

5. For a more detailed discussion of culture and tradition, see Frederick M. Barnard, "Culture and Civilization in Modern Times," in *Dictionary of the History of Ideas,* 5 vols. (New York: Scribner's, 1973), 1:613-21; and concerning "change" and "continuity," idem, "Natural Growth and Purposive Development: Vico and Herder," *History and Theory,* 18 (1979): 16-36.

6. Hobbes, *Leviathan* (New York: Dutton, 1950), pt. 1, chap. 14; see also part 2, chap. 21, pp. 106, 177.

7. See John Rawls, *A Theory of Justice* (Cambridge, Mass.: Harvard University Press, 1971), pp. 12, 19, and 136-42; Hannah Arendt, "What Is Freedom?" in *Between Past and Future* (New York: Viking, 1968), p. 169; idem, *The Human Condition* (Chicago: University of Chicago Press, 1958), pp. 222, 290. For a critical discussion of Arendt's position, see Frederick M. Barnard, "Infinity and Finality: Hannah Arendt on Politics and Truth," *Canadian Journal of Political and Social Theory* 1 (1977): 29-57.

8. For a philosophical-anthropological elaboration of this point, see J.G. Herder, *Ideas for a Philosophy of the History of Mankind,* book 9, in *Herder on Social and Political Culture,* ed. and trans. Frederick M. Barnard (London: Cambridge University Press, 1969), p. 312f.

9. For an extended discussion of manipulation in politics, see Robert E. Goodin, *Manipulatory Politics* (New Haven: Yale University Press, 1980), esp. pp. 13-14.

10. Among modern thinkers Herder was the first to see this close interdependence between the "outside" and the "inside" of our thinking and acting, symbolized, as it were, in human language (see esp. *Ideas for a Philosophy,* p. 141). On switching to a new language and the power of language to mold our pattern of thinking, see a most sensitive account by Arthur Koestler, *Bricks to Babel* (London: Hutchinson, 1980), pp. 218-19.

11. On an analysis of "two models" of man, a passive *plastic* man and an active *autonomous* man, see Martin Hollis, *Models of Man, Philosophical Thoughts on Social Action* (London: Cambridge University Press, 1977), esp. chap. 1.

12. Ernest Gellner captures Kant's anguish and intellectual honesty rather well in describing him as "a philosopher both of the ghost and of the

FREDERICK M. BARNARD

machine," since he is said to have had two fears, one for science, the
other for morality. The first fear was that the mechanical vision would
not hold; the second fear was that it *would*. Gellner sees Kant's greatness in that he felt *both* fears, yet "tolerated no facile arguments which
would play down their importance." See Gellner's *Legitimation of Belief*
(London: Cambridge University Press, 1974), p. 185.

13. Gyorgy Paloczi-Horvath, who took an active part in the Hungarian Revolution, knew all along of the lying and corruption in the party, of
its methods of extracting confessions, of the terror and the camps. He
knew how history was falsified and many more among the "thousands
of other facts my memory stored . . . about the elimination of whole
peoples and nations by the Kremlin leaders. Of course I knew everything." Yet the knowledge by itself did not move him to act for a long
time. See his *The Undefeated* (London: Secker and Warburg, 1959),
p. 191. I am indebted to Professor J.M. Porter, University of Saskatchewan, for having told me of this profoundly honest and penetrating
exploration of ideology, commitment, and utter cynicism.

14. See, for example, Kurt Baier in *The Moral Point of View* (Ithaca: Cornell
University Press, 1958).

15. I have discussed these points at some length in "Accounting for Actions:
Causality and Teleology," *History and Theory* 20 (1981): 291-312. For
the sake of brevity and (hopefully) tighter argument, I confine myself
here to "reasons for"; but I certainly neither dismiss nor belittle the
diverse and problematic forms of causality of "reasons from" as should
be evident from the article cited as well as from what I say here. Although I insist that both questions and answers are of a very different
order in each case, I concede that at times "reasons from" could be
redescribed as "reasons for" when, for example, "acting out of gratitude" may be said to be no different from "acting to show gratitude";
but I merely concede that this could be the case, not that it necessarily
is. Thus, I think it could be maintained that saying "I do this out of
gratitude" does not mean the same as saying "I do this to show gratitude." There is of course a fairly voluminous literature on these kinds
of distinctions. Useful bibliographies on the nature, description, and
explanation of action from a philosophical and sociological point of
view may be found in Alan R. White, ed., *The Philosophy of Action*
(London: Oxford University Press, 1968), pp. 167-71; and Glenn Lang-
ford, *Human Action* (Garden City, N.Y.: Doubleday, 1971), pp. 107-34.

16. Hannah Arendt, "Truth and Politics," in *Between Past and Future* (New
York: Viking, 1968), pp. 253-54.

17. Barnard, "Infinity and Finality," pp. 47-49. I do not dispute, of course,
that there might be neurotic states of more or less controlled schizo-
phrenia, conditioned reflexes, or, indeed, the total disintegration of personality, as Paloczi-Horvath reports (*The Undefeated*, p. 242). But this
does not, I think, alter the fact that the phrase "lying to oneself" is

a most problematical way of speaking, since it worryingly raises the question of the identity and continuity of the self.

18. David Hume, *Political Essays,* ed. C.W. Hendel (New York: Liberal Arts Press, 1953), p. 43,

19. Letter to Corcelle (16 October 1855), in Tocqueville, *Oeuvres et correspondance inédites,* 2:301, cited in Jack Lively, *The Social and Political Thought of Alexis de Tocqueville* (Oxford: Clarendon Press, 1962), pp. 58-59. In distinguishing political ideologies from all-encompassing belief systems or *Weltanschauungen* one also renders possible ideological differentiation *within* such systems. For example, there is no reason why an ideological style of politics, thus understood, could not exist within socialist systems, that is, in regimes committed to certain fundamental economic principles of production and distribution. Surely there is no logical or empirical basis for assuming that a socialist system—or any other broad belief system—could not (or in fact did not) give rise to more than one political party or faction, for an "ism" is clearly capable of being variously interpreted at different times or by different groups at any given time. I discuss this more fully (with R.A. Vernon) in "Socialist Pluralism and Pluralist Socialism," *Political Studies* 25 (1977): 477-90. It is of course not uncommon for a hiatus to exist between doctrinal principles and their operational use in day-to-day politics; nor is it unknown that, for a time at any rate, it can be effectively concealed or successfully played down, as the Austro-Marxists amply demonstrated. Sooner or later, however, the limits of pragmatic adaptation have to be borne in mind; for how "open," "flexible," or "weakly held" can principles get without ceasing to be principles? (I am referring here to Giovanni Sartori's categories in "Politics, Ideology, and Belief Systems," *American Political Science Review* 63 [1969]: 398-411.) There is a vast literature of widely differing quality on political ideology. A critical overview of much of it can be found in W.A. Mullins, "On the Concept of Ideology in Political Science," *American Political Science Review* 66 (1972): 498-510; and Martin Seliger, *Ideology and Politics* (London: Allen and Unwin, 1976).

20. *Discours prononcé à la séance publique annuelle* (3 Avril 1852) *de l'Académie des Sciences Morales et Politiques,* cited in Lively, *Social and Political Thought of de Tocqueville,* p. 61.

21. For an extended discussion of the epistemological considerations in the thinking of Tocqueville about political action, see Lively, p. 25. For his rather problematic views on revolutionary action, see John Stilborn, "Tocqueville and the Idea of Revolution" (Ph.D. diss., University of Western Ontario, 1979). The need for blending the general and the particular is well brought out in Brian Barry, *Political Argument* (London: Routledge, 1965), pp. 35-36.

22. Ludwig Wittgenstein, *Tractatus Logico-Philosophicus,* trans. D.F. Pears and B.F. McGuinnes (London: Routledge, 1961), p. 6.

23. I have touched (with R.A. Vernon) on the problem of multiple partial concerns and allegiances in "Pluralism, Participation, and Politics," *Political Theory* 3 (1975): 180-97.

24. If, as Robert Nozick (*Anarchy, State, and Utopia* [New York: Basic, Books 1974], p. 6) maintains, there are indeed only three possible ways of understanding the political realm, namely (1) in terms of the nonpolitical, (2) as emerging from the nonpolitical but irreducible to it, and (3) as something completely autonomous, I would opt for (1) in that I consider political and nonpolitical action to be structurally analogous. Thus, although I concede that the content and context could be decidedly at variance, I postulate a fundamental identity in morphology.

25. R.G. Collingwood, "Political Action," *Proceedings of the Aristotelian Society* 29 (1929): 158.

26. Significantly, a sense of measure or, more literally, a vision *containing* measure *(Augenmass)* Max Weber considered the quintessential tool for the vocational statesman or politician.

Commentary
Politics as Reasons in Action
J. M. PORTER

However politics is conceived, the activity itself would not be nourished and respected within a political system for long if human actions were held to be reducible to, and hence explainable by, causes independent of the actor's purported reasons, will, or intentions. For example, with some modern conceptions of politics the activity of politics is explained by recourse to undergirding interests. Hobbesians, utilitarians, or Marxists may well quarrel over the significance of one interest or group of interests versus another interest or set, but in any case a causal explanation, approximate or probable, is sought. The activities of ruling and decision making, as a consequence, can be viewed as matters requiring scientific knowledge and skills, albeit in a modern sense.[1] Within such a conceptual scheme political activity itself is, understandably, not nourished or respected since it is conceived of as a reflection of interests. It is, at best, a regrettable necessity. A political culture influenced by such conceptions of politics will have little respect for politicians and will come to think that "politics" is an aesthetically unpleasing reminder that the institutions and laws integral to the political system have not been properly tuned.

In contrast to thinking of politics as dissonance, one can, with Aristotle or the later Wittgenstein, view political activity as an activity not amenable to some a priori method of explanation and prediction, but as an activity constituted by the actor's reasons, will, or intentions.[2] Politics then becomes an activity for collective, public decisions and an activity that uses reasons in order to persuade. It is a difficult philosophic task to indicate that human action in general and political action in particular can be understood (i.e., made intelligible) through

65

an examination of the reasons of the actor and that human action is not captured by hypothetical-deductive strategies of explanation and prediction. A defense of politics, even if done with verve and common sense, will lose persuasive force if its philosophic flank is not well defended.[3] Thus it is appropriate that a political philosopher should explore the interplay of reasons and action. If, as Professor Barnard contends, reasons do play "an *essential* mediating role" and are "constitutive of what is said or done," then politics, a subspecies of human action, is not amenable to the diagnostic tools of a Hobbesian, utilitarian, or Marxist. Or, to phrase the point differently, the relation between *sophia* and *praxis* can be established through disclosing the nexus between reasons and action.

It is Professor Barnard's thesis that there can be a rational accounting for both individual action and joint action. The category of joint action includes, in Barnard's phrase, a politics of principles and beliefs or, to use an Aristotelian phrase, a politics of opinion or, in the nonpejorative sense, an ideological politics. There are, according to Barnard, analogous features between the two forms of action because they are derived from a common philosophic morphology. Just as reasons for an individual action are often viewed as rationalizations and determined in some manner, so too are political judgments and ideologies often viewed in contemporary political science. On the other hand, just as the individual can be conceived as self-directed, that is, as choosing to act for reasons and accounting for his actions within the context and limitations of external conditions, culture, and history, so too can the joint commitments of a political judgment or ideology be conceived. If Barnard's argument is sound about the reasons constituting action and about the common philosophic morphology of individual and political action, then new philosophic support would be provided for a politics of a public interest or of a politics of opinion, that is, a politics that is public and reasoned. The linchpin for this argument is Professor Barnard's views on the nature of reasoning, which must show how reasons are "contained" in actions and which must show the "causal efficacy" of reason.

There is a mass of literature that defends the distinction between events and actions and shows why reasons are a logical property of action. One of the best arguments for demonstrating the logical and conceptual gulf between events and actions is to note the loss of meaning that occurs when an action is described as an event. A wink, a blink, and a parody of a wink can all be identically described through physical and neurophysiological data and laws. The meaning of an act eludes such an explanatory net, and thus an action, inseparable from the reasons of the actor, is conceptually distinct from an event such as a blink.

Another method for demonstrating this gulf is to probe decision making or choosing. It is often noted that the manner in which an individual makes a decision or a choice cannot be *done* causally. When we are doing something such as making decisions, we are not, as Alan Ryan points out, "wondering what the possible causal explanation can be of why we make up our minds in the way we do," but we are wondering *"what is the right thing to do."*[4] Otherwise, no decision could ever be made. As a consequence, when examining another's action, we normally accept his account of the reasons for action as the explanation. Now it may be possible that the person is under a posthypnotic suggestion that caused him to act, but we have, at least implicitly, by such a use of "cause" noted that this kind of behavior is not normal human behavior.

Two features are worth noting here: A causal explanation based on physical and physiological laws is limited in its scope; and it is self-contradictory in cases other than, for example, psychotic personalities or posthypnotic suggestion, to ignore or deny reasons for acting in others that we accredit in our own case as an account and explanation of our actions. Human actions, and social relations in general, are not susceptible to a causal analysis in the way that the physical order is, as Barnard properly argues here, because human actions are meaningful actions, i.e., language and concepts are interwoven in such behavior. In short, in order to explain human actions the conceptual forms through which a human understands, and sometimes even performs, his actions must be part of the account.

It seems to me that Barnard's various arguments showing how reasons are contained in actions are sound. The second part of his case—the "causal efficacy" of reasons—is, in my judgment, also correctly argued except for one problematic segment. Whatever "causal efficacy" reason has, it cannot be conceived, as Barnard rightly insists, as a "mechanical operation" or a "natural process." He argues that reasons can have "causal efficacy only if they are understood, believed in, or accepted." Yet, while necessary, this too is not sufficient, as Barnard notes. A further distinction should be made between having reasons and minding reasons. Having reasons could well refer only to a post hoc rationalization, and having reasons as a ground for action may not commit one to act. Minding reasons evidently connotes an acceptance of the force of the reason, although, as Barnard quickly makes clear, even minding will not compel. His argument here resembles that of Stephen Toulmin: "In itself, a reason neither has, nor fails to have, causal efficacy: It is not a fact or event, but a consideration. What *can* have causal efficacy is the fact or event of a man's having, being given, recognizing, or acknowledging the force of, that reason."[5] In Toulmin's and Barnard's analyses the stress is on *can*. Unlike inevitable, mechanical causes, a reason for acting, while being an explanation and justification in a particular case and thereby having causal efficacy, need not be viewed as inevitable or imply that one could not have acted differently. Otherwise, words and arguments would "work" in this world as the Tibetan prayer wheels "work." Indeed, the power in the phrase "Here I stand, I can do no other!" is precisely that one, of course, could. In order to account for an action, the reasons must be entailed in the action; reasons are not the causal antecedents but the logical properties of the action. Thus, Barnard concludes, whether reasons were "there" (i.e., had causal efficacy) is a "question not of physical fact but of conceptual understanding."

The problematic segment of Barnard's argument can be found in his definition of rationality. It could be argued that his concept of rationality is not strong enough for its task. In a Peircean fashion, rationality is defined as a modality: "Beliefs—including political ideologies—have on this view a rational foundation if they are defensible or challengeable, if reasons in their support can be offered or demanded." He agrees that a reason for acting is intentional, but no particular substantive meaning is entailed. Given this conception of rationality, it seems difficult to explain, I argue, how reasons can *account* for actions and thus make them "explicable, discussable, and contestable."

Two cases can illustrate the difficulty. The devil's advocate could charge that a garrulous unicorn hunter could fulfill the requirement of a rational modality: The hunter could account for his actions and give reasons; he could discuss, defend, and contest in good faith. Another, perhaps more compelling, example can be found in E.E. Evans-Pritchard's famous study of the Azande people. These primitive people have no difficulty in rationally explaining and defending oracle beliefs. They too can defend, discuss, and contest at great length.[6] But, of course, such citing of "reasons" by the unicorn hunter and the Azande would have only the appearance of reasoning, however "reasonable" they may be. In fact, this is the problem: Modality on the surface cannot be distingished from, and is identical with, ersatz reasoning.

These examples are, in one sense, unfair. After all, the unicorn hunter and the Azande people are not truly taking part in a discussion in which there is, by our lights, real and rational contestation and explanation. When we insist on contestation as a sign of rationality, we mean "contestation" by the accepted canons of evidence and reason. Also, when we call for "giving reasons," we mean more, however difficult it may be to stipulate, than the internal consistency shown by the hunter and the Azande. Rational modality, if these qualifications are added, does have an implicit substantive dimension.

Such a dimension is required if there is to be an accounting through reasons for individual and joint action. Although Barnard properly maintains that acting for reasons cannot be viewed as analogous to "psychophysical or sociological causes" nor can acting for reasons be viewed as determined or reductively caused; unless "rational modality" is given some substantive meaning, the "reasons" that are logical properties of action will have little or no capacity for accounting. The "reasons" of the Azande or the unicorn hunter have no significant explanatory force. One needs to get behind the purported reasons in order to explain the behavior. In short, all reasons for action may have the same structural-conceptual form, but their capacity for accounting for action will vary tremendously precisely because of the substantive content of the reasons of the actor.

The problematic feature of a nonsubstantive conception of rationality also troubles Barnard's careful analysis of causal efficacy. Briefly, reasons with regard to action and political ideology with regard to joint political action provide, we are told, causal efficacy. This type of cause, as Barnard makes clear, is different from socioeconomic or psychophysical causes: "For reasons (and meanings) possess a cognitive status of their own independently of their nonrational genesis." When such reasons within a belief become a commitment, a political ideology becomes "action-promoting." The problem is in detecting when a reason as a belief becomes a reason as a commitment, and action ensues. There is, he says, no "specific property in reasons themselves that qualifies them either as reasons qua beliefs or as reasons qua commitments." And, he continues, "nor can I—rather regretfully—see what difference it makes to the switch from mere belief to actual commitment if it results from authentic information and experience rather than from people being deliberately fed with lies; for the causal efficacy of the switch seems wholly independent of the nature of its genesis." This seems indubitably true. Yet, again, there is a crucial difference if one is to account for action, including political action. In the case of lies, the political ideology that is so formed and that becomes action-promoting (i.e., has causal efficacy) could not account for the political action. It would be of little relevance to refer to the meanings and independent cognitive status of such "reasons" for action. One should resort to socioeconomic or psychophysical causes. Does this not mean that the "action," then, was in reality an "event"? Some substantive sense appears to be necessary if reasons can be said to have causal efficacy.

Notes

1. Richard E. Flathman, *The Public Interest: An Essay Concerning the Normative Discourse of Politics* (New York: Wiley, 1966); Virginia Held, *The Public Interest and Individual Interest* (New York: Basic Books, 1970).
2. John W. Danford, *Wittgenstein and Political Philosophy: A Reexamination of the Foundations of Social Science* (Chicago: University of Chicago Press, 1978).
3. Bernard R. Crick, *In Defence of Politics* (Chicago: University of Chicago Press, 1978).
4. Alan Ryan, *The Philosophy of the Social Sciences* (London: Macmillan, 1970), p. 118.
5. Stephen Toulmin, "Reasons and Causes," as found in *Explanation in the Behavioral Sciences,* ed. Robert Borger and Frank Cioffi (New York: Cambridge University Press, 1970), p. 20.
6. E.E. Evans-Pritchard, *Witchcraft, Oracles, and Magic Among the Azande* (Oxford: Oxford University Press, 1937). See the discussion by Michael Polanyi, *Personal Knowledge: Towards a Post-Critical Philosophy* (Chicago: University of Chicago Press, 1958), pp. 287-92.

GEORGE J. GRAHAM, JR.
AND
WILLIAM C. HAVARD, JR.

The Language of the Statesman: Philosophy and Rhetoric in Contemporary Politics

3

Political discourse unguided by reason in its full classical dimension is merely ideologically based hyperbole and thus a potentially dangerous means of motivating political action. In attempting to establish the proper relation between political knowledge and action, of bringing *sophia* to bear on *praxis* as it were, it becomes clear that the connection is especially weak when seen from the modern perspective.

Since the latter half of the eighteenth century, at least, the dominant epistemological creed has been some—not always clearly articulated—version of positivism. Immanuel Kant's separation of knowledge into the categories of "pure" and "practical" reason, while heuristically useful for identifying the different modes of experience appertaining to the sciences of natural phenomena and the sciences of man and society, capped a long historical trend toward the subsumption of all knowledge that could claim the validity of truth by the methods of the natural sciences.

In some respects this development resolved the late medieval, early Renaissance controversy between the nominalists and the exponents of reality in favor of the nominalist position on ontological issues. Epistemic validity was thus limited to those things that could be apprehended through the senses and abstractly described (both in their static conditions and in the processes of change) through quantitative symbolization.

GEORGE J. GRAHAM, JR. AND WILLIAM C. HAVARD, JR.

The Modern Context and the Need
for Improved Political Discourse

The late Richard M. Weaver argued that the widespread adoption of this "modern" conception of knowledge produced no less than "an alteration of man's image of man," with the new perspective being best described as " 'scientistic,' a term which denotes the application of scientific assumptions to subjects which are not wholly comprised of naturalistic phenomena." In face of successful results of scientific applications in "changing the landscape and revolutionizing the modes of industry" it was easy to infer that men ought increasingly to become scientists and arrive at the derivative opinion that man "at his best is a logic machine." A further consequence was that those aspects of man that characterized his humanity—rationality that is more than logic, emotionality (the capacities for feeling and suffering, for knowing pleasure, for aesthetic satisfaction), and the religious impulse—fell into disparagement.[1]

Even though such a view of man reduced mind to a phenomenon of nature and reason to an instrumentalist capacity to order the analysis of discrete properties of things according to deductive laws that would be affirmed in their generality by further observation, and therefore relegated all other forms of experience to the realms of contingency or idle metaphysical speculation on the unknowable, such scientific knowledge was viewed in a way that appears to contain an unacknowledged paradox, as a source of power (in Bacon's terms), which in extending itself would eventually enable all contingency to be overcome by man's progressive capacity to control nature and society. Thus all knowledge became instrumental, and the sciences of man and society that dealt with questions of being and existence, justice and right order, consciousness and human experience, history and the struggle for personal and social order were no longer regarded as seeking "useful" knowledge (following the categorization employed by the French Encyclopedists). Considerations of what constituted proper ends and universal goods yielded to the use of knowledge as power applied to the structuring of nature and society in a way that would fulfill

74

the vague promise of satisfying all our wants. The power to control or dominate nature (including human nature) was substituted for the ethical and political problem of the application of reason to the apprehension of an order of goods that provides for the closest approximation possible to the satisfaction of human needs, to the inevitable making of choices among alternatives in full recognition of natural and human potential and limits, and to the persuasion of the body politic of the validity of goods and choices and the proper means to their realization. The problems of complete separation of object and subject, absolute distinctions between facts and values and the abrogation of the search for rational meaning in human existence (T.S. Eliot's "dissociation of sensibility," or alienation from self, humanity, and God) emerge from this displacement of *noesis* by instrumental reason. The relation between *sophia* and *praxis* in the practical areas of ethics and politics is rendered nugatory by this radical lobotomy of the human spirit.

Although Immanuel Kant is perhaps the most frequently cited source for this condition of treating knowledge as instrumental, most modern analysts must share the responsibility for devaluing the relation of knowledge to political action in ethical terms. Man discovered "values" in essence in the objects of his appetitive passions and permitted himself in the uncontrolled pursuit of these "goods" to be devoured by them. Most Western intellectuals today, through commitment to the artificial separation of factual and evaluative understandings, have rediscovered (and taught) "vulgar conventionalism" only to reconstruct abstract values as universals, establishing entitlements to ungrounded rights without cognizance of the fact that their reconstructions are merely formalization of ideological conventions as abstract truths.[2] It is enough to note that John Rawls' brilliant use of instrumental reason merely provides an abstract formula for the way the ideological conventions of an egalitarian liberal regime can be transformed almost magically into human rights (with entitlements) without — intentionally without — considerations of either human consciousness or human experience. Both the substance of consciousness and reflection on the cumulative accretion of historical experience are obscured

75

by his well-designated veil of ignorance.[3] The fact that Rawls' language of entitlements and the centrality of categorical rights, with little or no consideration of the necessity for the establishment of correlative obligations, have become part of contemporary Western political discourse illustrates well the crisis of modern politics.

If modern philosophy fails to provide guidance in relating *sophia* to *praxis,* modern social science—especially in its enthusiasm for its latest fad of public policy analysis—falls essentially into the instrumentalist trap. Aaron Wildavsky, a leading figure in the field, identifies the central activity of policy analysis as "creating problems that can be solved."[4] Purely opportunistic in orientation, then, he permits accidents of availability—governmental interests and funding—to guide one's applications. This purposeless approach to analysis often leads to the "discovery" of researchable policy topics, which can then be designated, in almost perfect congruence with Edward Banfield's discerning characterization in "Policy Science as Metaphysical Madness," a public policy problem.[5] Here the instrumentalist reason employed in an analytics deliberately preempted of political meaning creates public policy problems that can then be solved by following the instrumentalist's prescription from the analysis. An illusion of success is created as one, following Wildavsky, finds data that fit the instrument in a fashion close to Abraham Kaplan's law of the instrument: "Give a small boy a hammer and he will find that everything he encounters needs pounding."[6] In fairness to the policy analyst, especially Wildavsky, we will later return to this point to show that classical rhetoric can implicitly provide a framework for his own views of the art and craft of policy analysis by connecting instrumental policy analysis to proper ends established by political discourse.

Given these epistemological presuppositions and their practical consequences, it is a relatively simple task to make a general case against the current languages of political discourse. Campaign rhetoric tends to be almost exclusively instrumental, designed solely to secure access to office. Given the techniques available for ascertaining the psychological dispositions of the voters and for calculating the geographic distribution of probable voting responses in order to attain maximum returns relative to the arrangements of electoral districts and the other factors affecting electoral outcomes, it is not surprising that the rhetorical strategy should be directed to evoking, through both overt and subliminal appeals, those elemental appetites, desires, and aversions discerned in the analysis of survey and aggregate data, as well as to employing the techniques of commercial advertising. The other principal motivational appeal (in this case in response to previously ascertained perceptions by voters of the personal qualities of candidates) is made through the creation of an image of personality and character compatible with the composite public expectation of leadership traits. Once in office, and presumably vested with its responsibilities, the politician's rhetorical appeals to political action shift from the focus on the voter approbation needed to secure office to the persuasive effort (directed at a different set of constituencies) required to frame and implement public policy. And here the prevailing tendency seems to be to temporize by means of a forceful articulation of clichés, fully agreeing with everything that has been said on all sides of a question, in the apparent hope (in the United States, at least) that the Supreme Court by a timely ex cathedra pronouncement from the throne of higher law, will remove the essential moral issues from the realm of politics before the politician has to make a public commitment on them.

The glittering generality, the quick-fix comprehensive solution, and the sweeping promise camouflage the practice of buying off the proliferating brokers who mobilize malcontents around any convenient symbol of ostensible common interests. It is small wonder that such a hollow rhetoric contributes to the sense of malaise ascribed by former President Carter to the American body politic, and in a more direct way to a politics of disaggregation featuring single-interest groups whose discrete demands are directed to bureaucrats whose "public" obligations (not to speak of ambitions) are fulfilled entirely by service to these particularistic groups. These patterns of human interaction are in turn aided and abetted by those predominant forces in the academy who are at ease speaking the instrumental language of the so-called behavioral sciences with their indulgence in the naturalistic fallacy and restriction of "pure" knowledge to the sciences of external phenomena. Modern political language thus condemns itself by its very structure.

The language of the Statesman, by contrast with that of the politician as "office seeker" and "policy advocate," has never been more badly needed, nor more conspicuous by its absence, than in contemporary democratic regimes, which are in dire need of reaching beyond the struggle for satisfying individual and group interest demands for utilities in a setting that decries principled argument. The voices of wisdom seem increasingly overwhelmed by the echoes of vocal interests justifying their wants by abstract images of universal rights. Were the claims of rights grounded in human experience, the Statesman could join them in serious discourse.

Our argument is simple: Political discourse requires rhetoric if it is to become, as it was for Aristotle, the language of the Statesman. But the language of the Statesman, considered as one worthy to rule as distinguished from the political activist or politician per se, is not *mere rhetoric* but rhetoric grounded in ontological truth noetically apprehended and therefore directed toward proper ends in the conduct of moral and political relations among human beings. To treat political rhetoric as a discrete subject apart from the science of politics is to commit the fallacy of misplaced concreteness, since rhetoric bears a relation to the initiation of political action that is similar to what the dialectic does in the philosophical apprehension of moral and political knowledge. In the realm of practical discourse rhetoric provides a *method* that should be considered an art in the service of a science rather than a thing complete in itself that becomes a serviceable tool for any proximate purpose informed by immediate political desire. Its status as an art is neutral. The Statesman needs to know the art of rhetoric as a means of persuasion that induces political activity. But what is more important is that the Statesman ground this art in ends established by the appropriate human sciences, which for Aristotle meant the sciences of ethics and politics. Once we review these complex relationships in order to comprehend the end of political rhetoric for the Statesman, and its essential educational function, it becomes possible to focus on the coherence of *sophia* and *praxis* in political discourse. Only after having established the positive connections among philosophical knowledge, deliberation, education, and action can we explore the possibility of linking philosophy and rhetoric in contemporary politics.

Aristotle's Structure of Deliberative Political Discourse

Aristotle introduces the subject with which the Statesman, or the true legislator, ought to be acquainted as a complex but related set of comprehensions: The science of politics must apprehend not only the best regime in general with no contextual limits but also the best possible regime relative to historical contexts as well as those that can be constituted pragmatically in particular circumstances.[7] This comprehension demands of the Statesman a sensitivity to the conditions found in any and every political setting and the method necessary for developing convincing recommendations based on his understanding of the best regime and the possible ones. That is, prescriptions for action are grounded in experience, but are guided by the standards of knowledge of politics as a universal human activity serving complex human needs. *Praxis* for the Statesman, then, refers not to practice simply understood, but to the sense of "Performing the activity well: *'eupraxia.'*"[8] Theoretical knowledge of politics sets the standards for prescribing appropriate action; the science of politics defines the end of instrumental applications even when the focus becomes immediate remedies for defects under existing regimes. Thus, for the Statesman, Aristotle demands that difficult but special mode of practice found only by conjoining *sophia* and *praxis*. The skillful use of language to evoke political activity at its purposive best becomes his method.

Rhetoric, for Aristotle, is an art rather than a science, though a rather special art as adapted for the use of the Statesman. Unlike our current denigrating use of the term "rhetoric" to attack the misleading oratorial embellishments of political foes, which use has debased the very idea of rhetoric as a practical art for communicating truth in a form congruent with the experience of those it reaches, and has led to its decline as an appropriate area of study in the humanities, or even in contrast with the open definition of Quintilian that rhetoric is the "science of speaking well,"[9] Aristotle treats rhetoric as "the faculty of discovering in the particular case what are the available means of persuasion. . . . [T]he art as such has no special application to any distinct class of subjects."[10] The art is neutral as to (internal) content, just as a logical syllogism is neutral within dialectics. The important distinction between Aristotle and latter belletristic students of rhetoric—Quintilian, Cicero, Hugh Blair, among others—is found in the fact that rhetoric for each side is a key to a different lock. For Aristotle it is an art to be placed in the service of an artist; that is, rhetoric is for Aristotle a means in the service of truth, while for the others it is an end in itself serving only the practitioner.[11] In this distinction itself one discovers the *praxis* of a classical truth.

This point is meant to convey a deeper importance than its surface patency. Without rhetorical skills it is unclear that one has the means for translating political and ethical knowledge into *praxis* at all. Unlike Plato, Aristotle does not provide mythic symbols as a holistic expression of his political philosophy that can be apprehended by his audience. Instead, Aristotle presents his theory as theory in the language symbols applicable to philosophical discourse. His theory stands ready to be employed in practice much as it has been framed in understanding. At first one wonders how such comprehensive and detailed expositions could be presented without a corresponding articulation of *praxis;* his theories are an interrelated series of standards guided by explications of natural ends. Until the questions associated with *praxis* are raised, the philosopher in us is certainly happy to share in the activity of understanding reality as it is articulated in his sciences of ethics and politics. It is only through reading backward from the *Rhetoric* to the *Politics* and the *Ethics* that the full force of the cohesive structure of his thought emerges. Rhetoric is treated as an important communicative extension of *noesis* rather than, as it often seems in Plato, its mortal enemy, because for Aristotle rhetoric is a necessary means of fulfilling the political role of the Statesman. It provides a method of transition from *episteme* to *praxis* in two ways: It permits the working out of applications of universal propositions in the context of contextual problematics—which deal with uncertainties and probabilities—and it provides the means of educating the public in nonideal contexts that demand good habits with the best possible rational comprehension of why those habits are good. Not only is rhetoric a means of translating the sciences of ethics and politics for the public, but, properly understood, rhetoric is the only means to such translation. Rhetoric is thus the means of proper continuous political education of the citizens.

The importance of "audience" in Aristotle's conception of rhetoric draws our attention even more strongly to the educational role of rhetoric.[12] As an art, rhetoric seeks to develop persuasive arguments. In the search for the best answers in the arena of uncertainty and probable knowledge—of practical application of *episteme* as confronted by the Statesman in applying political and ethical knowledge—rhetoric becomes important in both its deliberative and its persuasive-educative aspects: Testing all possible arguments while exploring the many potential consequences and simultaneously engaging in assessments of commitments on the part of the audience, the Statesman shares deliberative discourse with his audience in the search for and the reasons for both developing and accepting appropriate prescription for *praxis*. In addition, the exploration of consequences permits the audience to share in the rational assessment of long-range consequences that inevitably proscribe many desires for immediate satiation by reasons of demonstrating the merits of temperance and moderation. The successful rhetor, even if seeking merely to deliberate concerning the best possible prescription for action from among options, reasons aloud, as it were, before an audience, permitting at least vicarious participation by the audience in the reasoning. Aristotle not only considered that the rhetor served truth best by pursuing rational over emotive appeal but he also made two corollary points: Reasoned argument is more persuasive than emotive (a point on method), and the rhetor best uses emotive persuasive skills to prepare the audience for rational argument (a point on *both* method *and* education).[13]

The shift from Plato's position on rhetoric was, in a valid sense, a means of taking rhetoric away from the Sophists. No matter how these teachers of grammar, rhetoric, and dialectic varied in their particular emphases, they shared in one common pursuit as they "educated" young men whose goals of advancing themselves would inevitably lead them into the political life of their city-states; the Sophists taught the "*techne* that would encourage clear, effective, and persuasive thought and speech."[14] Gorgias, for example, was a Sophist who wrote one of the early handbooks on rhetoric, yet he advanced such ontic and epistemic propositions as "nothing exists" and "if anything exists, it is incomprehensible."[15] It is no wonder that Plato found it necessary with his students, who were of the same background as those attracted by personal political motives to training in rhetoric, to counter the Sophists by defining reasoning in pursuit of truth against reasoning as *techne,* whose only ends appear to be public power and control. Plato distinguished dialectic from rhetoric in order to preserve philosophy; Aristotle distinguished the two in order to place rhetoric in the service of philosophy. Insofar as our highest human experience is doing philosophy together (according to Aristotle's *Ethics*), we are able to avoid the *Rhetoric.* Insofar as the philosopher's responsibility leads to the practice of politics, the highest of the sciences, rhetoric becomes the *techne* of *praxis.* Thus, knowing all available means of persuasion (rational and emotional) becomes a necessary first step in the Statesman's approach to *praxis.*

This transformation of rhetoric from a weapon of the enemies of the noetic virtues to their service does not raise *techne* to equal status with the guiding sciences. The ends of the sciences are paramount:

> Now it would seem that this supreme End must be the object of the most authoritative of the sciences—some science which

is preeminently a master-craft. But such is manifestly the science of Politics; for it is this that ordains which of the sciences are to exist in states and what branches of knowledge the different classes of the citizens are to learn and up to what point; and we observe that even the most highly esteemed of the faculties, such as strategy, domestic economy, oratory, are subordinate to the political science.[16]

What does change is our focus on proper use of rhetoric. Aristotle turns us from the question whether one ought to pursue philosophy *or* rhetoric to the question of how to employ the inferior in the service of the superior; in application, as in science, the methods or means subserve the substance rather than the other way around.

The special attention to reason within rhetoric is found in all of Aristotle's related works. In *Posterior Analytics,* he establishes all uses of reason and education as proceeding out of preexisting knowledge, moving with syllogism or induction from either an intelligent audience's presumed assumptions or an acceptance of universal self-evidence of particulars. He argues that rhetorical arguments proceed the same way, employing enthymemes as a kind of syllogism and examples as induction.[17] In *Topics,* Aristotle compares rhetoric and medicine as arts that *can* be practiced without pursuing every expedient, but either, if possessed adequately, would omit no means of its practice.[18] Indicative of Aristotle's intent here is the fact that rhetoric is persuasion, but must be viewed as an activity that has to employ *all* means of persuasion, including reasoning. Moreover, in education especially, the student already possesses the materials of thought, so to speak, which will receive guidance by dialectics and rhetoric. The teacher will need to employ all means of persuasion in order to prepare the student for receiving rational, deliberative presentations, that is, to be persuaded by them.[19]

An important point concerning *the public* and its *education* in the *Politics* enhances the importance of rhetoric to the Statesman. Much of Book VI of the *Politics* deals with the importance of the preservation of the state once it is established. This means, of course, continuous efforts to maintain the proper understandings whether in practical deliberation or in education. Because changing contexts confront the citizens with exigencies unforeseen in the best of laws, the role of deliberative rhetoric is continuous and may actually lead to contrary practical conclusions flowing from a single general law. This problem of translating a general principle to fit a changing context is perhaps the most difficult task for the rhetor, because both previous rationalizations and emotional commitments must be challenged by effective persuasion. And if particular laws must be reversed, education to good habits is made more difficult by the need to counter the charge of pure expediency, whether dealing with the young in age or mind or altering long-held traditions. (This is why Aristotle sees good reason not to change to a better standard of law when only trivial improvement is involved.) The point is simple, though it deserves more extensive treatment than we can give it here: *Praxis* must be steadily pursued if it is to achieve its end; it must be engaged continuously in adapting the particular to the general in changing contexts.

Rhetoric, then, is the key to *praxis* properly understood. It translates philosophy, which is grounded in human experience as a whole, into a form of understanding conveyed to the audience because of their human experiences and their capacity for *noesis* as a human attribute, at least to the point of grasping by means of common sense the foundations in truth of those things communicated by the philosopher-statesman, even if the role of the citizen-participant is not that of the philosopher. Rhetoric can be employed to reason about, draw attention to, and dramatically suggest those experiences out of which knowledge is obtained through deductive and inductive reasoning by the human sciences that utilize the dialectic to probe to the rational foundations themselves. But rhetoric cannot be employed independently of a grasp of the meaning and limits of human consciousness and a comprehension of the way it apprehends what the philosopher can know of reality because these human experiences and capacities, provided to the rhetor in raw form by an audience, set the framework for discourse. Understanding this, Aristotle provides the complete art of persuasion to

84

the Statesman so that the nonrational appeals can permit him to prepare the audience for rational deliberation. And rational argument, in the context of the human constraints, is the most persuasive of all forms of rhetorical appeal.[20]

Can Contemporary Politicians Be Statesmen?

The centrality of context and audience to the art of persuasion is important in comprehending the political role of the Statesman. The importance of audience is found in the need to begin with shared beliefs and symbols in the public consciousness of the participants. Good habits and the beliefs of those who listen permit the rhetor to guide them, through expedience, toward such ends as truth and justice even though rhetoric is an instrumental good.[21] The end of deliberative rhetoric becomes the good.

> Let good be defined as that which is chosen in and for itself;
> or as that for which we choose something else; or that which
> is desired by all beings, or by all sentient beings, or beings with
> intelligence, or that which would be desired by anything that
> acquired intelligence.[22]

This comprehension permits one to recognize that rhetoric provides the Statesman with the instrument to treat deliberative argument as the means of translating *sophia* into *praxis* within the context of an audience that can see, through expedience, how their experiences plus argument can lead to the best possible settlements within politics.

The role of deliberative political argument from Aristotle, then, parallels with one exceptional difference the presentation of Stephen Toulmin's conceptions of ethics-in-use as the effort "to correlate our feelings and behavior in such a way as to make the fulfillment of everyone's aims and desires [within a community] as far as possible compatible."[23] The difference with Aristotle is that the latter sees the discourse not merely as an instrument for compromise but as the mechanism for achieving the best approximation of the good. The difference may be captured by Aristotle's recognition of the virtue of *phronesis,* or practical wisdom.[24]

The role of rhetoric in advancing discussion toward higher purposes is not impossible if one maintains a focus on ends rather than means; the sense that politics as usual, based on power distributions and interests, is beyond the scope of rhetoric misses the educational dimension of argument. Just as James Madison argued that deliberative leadership could "suspend the blow mediated by the people against themselves, until reason, justice, and truth can regain their authority over the public mind,"[25] Richard Weaver points out that the lack of deliberation and principled opposition can lead "a party to positions where it has no policy, or only a policy of opposing an incumbent."[26] Reason, truth, and justice require, for support of an audience, a rhetoric searching for proper principles acceptable to the audience. In discussing the American Whig party, Weaver says:

> But a party whose only program is an endorsement of the *status quo* is destined to go to pieces whenever the course of events brings a principle strongly to the fore. . . . As always occurs in such crises, the compromises are regarded as unreliable by both sides and are soon ejected from the scene.[27]

Weaver points us toward the reason that we can trust Madison's sense of responsible leadership: The public looks to principle when contexts require a shift from usual politics. Therefore, when incremental interest politics reaches a crisis, Statesmen can arise with common sense providing the common ground for the Statesman and the citizen.

Though we are apprehensive about the connotations entailed in his selection of language (especially the use of the term "transforming") to make the distinction, Weaver touches upon James MacGregor Burns' separation of types of leadership into

> the *transactional* and the *transforming.* The relations of most leaders and followers are transactional—leaders approach followers with an eye to exchanging one thing for another: jobs for votes, or subsidies for campaign contributions. Such transactions comprise the bulk of the relationships among leaders

and followers, especially in groups, legislatures, and parties. *Transforming* leadership, while more complex, is more potent. The transforming leader recognizes and exploits an existing need or demand of a potential follower. But beyond that, the transforming leader looks for potential motives in followers, seeks to satisfy higher needs, and engages the full person of the follower. The result of transforming leadership is a relationship of mutual stimulation and elevation that converts followers into leaders and may convert leaders into moral agents.[28]

The only instrument for Burns' transformational leader is, of course, rhetoric, but it is not treated by Burns as more than an instrument. Burns must be supplemented by the older vision of Hans J. Morgenthau:

> Politics must be understood through reason, yet it is not in reason that it finds its model. The principles of scientific reason are always simple, consistent, and abstract; the social world is always complicated, incongruous, and concrete. To apply the former to the latter is either futile, in that the social reality remains impervious to the attack of that "one-eyed reason, deficient in its vision of depth"; or it is fatal, in that it will bring about results destructive of the intended purpose. Politics is an art and not a science, and what is required for its mastery is not the rationality of the engineer but the wisdom and the moral strength of the statesman. The social world, deaf to the appeal to reason pure and simple, yields only to that intricate combination of moral and material pressures which the art of the statesman creates and maintains.[29]

As one sorts through the exigencies of politics today, the negative is omnipresent in our considerations, but we must avoid overlooking the obvious combinations of *sophia* and *praxis* that are achieved as we commiserate over the pedestrian. Not only can we imagine the possibility of a Statesman in our current political context, it is impossible not to imagine this possibility if we take Weaver seriously. Indeed, American candidates for Statesman in recent decades were masters of the very electronic media often identified as the cause of failure of modern rhetoricians. Three candidates who might qualify as Statesman, and their problems, are President Franklin D. Roosevelt, who

87

confronted the task of redefining an extended role for government in the face of two crises; the Reverend Martin Luther King, Jr., who was faced with the problem of moving Blacks to the political action needed to fulfill the promise of equal justice for all emphasized in the American political creed while maintaining the constraints on political means required to forestall counteractions that might have frustrated the civil rights movement entirely; and President Ronald Reagan, who appears to be trying to face up to the problem of reinvigorating a society in which cumulative dissatisfactions, moral uncertainties, and economic and social stagnation constitute a latent crisis that has been smoldering for nearly two decades.

Roosevelt used the newly available electronic media so skillfully that persons of the right age vividly recall the sense of personal or small-group (community) intimacy that he achieved in the fireside chats. He assuaged fear by his direct appeal to avoid either panic or paralysis by fearing fear itself more than the problems that were to be confronted. He not only convinced the citizenry that he was engaged in the effort to save the political tradition in which the experience of public life in America was rooted but he also pointed out the responsibilities of the various social and economic groups in relation to the tasks that confronted the nation, and he gained acceptance for the experiments in programs and their management that provided the flexibility to work out pragmatic solutions as problems arose and then translate those that proved effective into more lasting efforts.

The public has no difficulty grasping the complex import of his metaphors, such as "pump priming," because they shared the language that enabled an action at an elemental physical level to evoke a concept that could be applied to a far more complex economic and political problem. As the crisis shifted from domestic matters to international politics, he employed the same rhetorical skills used to expand the governmental role in domestic affairs to meet the needs of a matured industrial economy that was no longer a self-sustaining, self-correcting system to the redefinition of America's role in an international politics that had run amuck.

King was a master of oratorical rhetoric who is perhaps best characterized by the remark of an older political scientist who, after hearing him in the late 1950s, remarked that he was the finest political speaker he had heard since William Jennings Bryan, but that, unlike Bryan's, Dr. King's speech had substance. The substance was a call to his white audience to honor their obligations to those principles that were part of their political heritage, and his appeals (both to ends and to the peaceful means to their realization) were to universal principles in a context of limits and potentials that reflected the reality of a divided society that needed to be annealed. To the Blacks his calls for action were always tempered by prudential constraint and by reminders that they, too, were part of the religious and political community at large, although still not sharing all of its benefits and responsibilities.

Reagan, of course, is still in the process of "becoming" rather than "being" a Statesman. But the signs of principled argument are there, not only in his positive rhetoric, but also in the strength of his resistence to some of his most vociferous "total solution" supporters (and sometime critics). He has made it clear that he is engaged in the effort to redress the perceived imbalance in the distribution of functions in the public and private sectors, as well as among the various levels of government, in response to what may be characterized as the post-industrial era of slowed economic growth, limited resources, inflation, government overload, and the failure of so many specific programs to fulfill the promise of coping with unemployment, problems of urban life, welfare, health care, and so forth, by means of massive public expenditures and bloated bureaucracies. Like both Roosevelt and King, Reagan is not afraid to tell the audience some "negative truths" that need to be confronted. His rhetorical skills, rationally applied, appear to have created a public (and even congressional) receptivity that may enable his specific policies to be framed and implemented in ways that will give them a chance to work toward the realization of the larger ends. The main question that is still unanswered is whether Reagan places too much reliance on a literal return to the classical individualism (libertarianism) of an earlier era, and therefore may not be able to adapt abiding principles to the altered conditions of the times.

Because the differences in their respective policy means are so obvious, some will be reluctant to compare Reagan and Roosevelt, even in matters of rhetorical style and substance. But in the matters of dealing with a crisis by appeals to the experience of the American public within a political tradition that reflects a common understanding of the nature of political good, and the capacity to adapt the pursuit of that good to a particular time and circumstance, what is common to their understanding and to their mode of communicating that understanding to the public seems far greater than those things on which they might be divided. Above all, the similarity of their use of rhetoric (and Dr. King's as well, though his position and role were not those of a President) reflects a theory of politics that is purposive in the right sense and not merely instrumental, and the rhetoric itself indicates two further defining characteristics of the Statesman that have been reinforced throughout this paper: (1) an awareness that rhetoric is in practical service to political knowledge, and (2) that rhetoric is best directed to securing public acceptance for political *praxis* when its persuasive appeals are directed principally to the reason of the citizen. As a mature human being, the citizen shares with the Statesman not only the experience that derives from participation in the political tradition but in a larger dimension has a developed common sense that is noetically based. It is this noetic potential in the citizen to which the Statesman's appeal may be addressed in the expectation that the latter's grounding of practice in political *episteme* (i.e., *phronesis*) will be understood, at least to the extent that the Statesman can be trusted with a public mandate to translate *sophia* into political *praxis*.

Notes

1. In the collection of Weaver's essays on rhetoric, *Language Is Sermonic,* ed. Rich L. Johannesen, Rennard Strickland, and Ralph T. Eubanks (Baton Rouge: Louisiana State University Press, 1970), pp. 203-4.
2. Leo Strauss, *Natural Right and History* (Chicago: University of Chicago

Press, 1953), pp. 114-19. See also, passim, but especially chap. 4 where Strauss focuses on the consequences of distinguishing between external, rationalistic assessment of values as against the philosopher's pursuit of *nous* in its applications to human consciousness. The former seems characteristic of many modern instrumentalistic rationalists.

3. John Rawls, *A Theory of Justice* (Cambridge, Mass.: Harvard University Press, 1971), pp. 17-22. In a sense, Rawls reduces to a materialistic theory of interest politics.

4. *Speaking Truth to Power: The Art and Craft of Policy Analysis* (Boston: Little, Brown, 1979), p. 17. The emphasis on creating problems (passim) is especially telling in another of his explications at pp. 15-16: "Policy analysis must create problems that decision-makers are able to handle with the variables under their control and in the time available." This instrumentalistic assessment takes on more meaning when placed into the context of Wildavsky's earlier comment, "Cold comfort; those who can't say what it is, teach and those who can do policy analysis, still can't say how it is possible to do it" (p. 2). In contrast, one can find solace from the moderns in Ludwig Wittgenstein's good sense in recommending to those in a scientific language game that they remain silent about that which they cannot speak; see *Tractatus Logico-Philosophicus,* trans. D.F. Pears and B.F. McGuinness (New York: Humanities Press, 1961), p. 151.

5. Robert Goldwin, ed., *Bureaucrats, Policy Analysts, Statesmen: Who Leads?* (Washington, D.C.: American Enterprise Institute, 1980), pp. 1-19.

6. *The Conduct of Inquiry: Methodology for Behavioral Science* (San Francisco: Chandler, 1964), p. 28.

7. *Politics* IV. i. 1288b21-1289a25.

8. Richard J. Bernstein, *Praxis and Action: Contemporary Philosophy of Human Action* (Philadelphia: University of Pennsylvania Press, 1971), p. x. Bernstein's analysis of classical *praxis* in studying contemporary theorists of human action should be read in conjunction with Nicholas Lobkowicz, *Theory and Practice: History of a Concept from Aristotle to Marx* (Notre Dame: University of Notre Dame Press, 1967).

9. *Institutio Oratoria,* trans. H.E. Butler (London, 1953), p. 319.

10. *The Rhetoric of Aristotle,* trans. Lane Cooper (Englewood Cliffs, N.J.: Prentice-Hall, 1932), pp. 7-8.

11. Wayne D. Fields, "Rhetorical Theory and Political Argument" (paper presented to the Foundations of Political Theory Group, American Political Science Association meeting, Washington, D.C., 1 September 1977), explores the distinctions between the styles of rhetoric and explores the irony that the early American statesmen pursued deliberative rhetoric whereas they were pulled by Blair's texts toward belletristic rhetoric.

12. Audience is essentially determinative of success in persuasion no matter whether the persuasion arises from the character of the speaker, from the emotions of hearers, or by reasoning (see *Rhetoric,* pp. 8-9). In-

deed, the nature of the audience sets the end or purpose of the speech (*Rhetoric,* p. 16).

13. On this point, Aristotle is clear: "But the art of Rhetoric has its value. It is valuable, first because truth and justice are by nature more powerful than their opposites, so that, when decisions are not made as they should be, the speakers with right on their side have only themselves to thank for the outcome. Their neglect of the art needs correction . . . it is characteristic of Rhetoric and Dialectic alone that, abstractly considered, they may indifferently prove opposite statements. Still, their basis, in the facts, is not a matter of indifference, for, speaking broadly, what is true and preferable is by nature always easier to prove, and more convincing" (*Rhetoric,* pp. 5-6).

14. William Anderson, *Man's Quest for Political Knowledge: The Study and Teaching of Politics in Ancient Times* (Minneapolis: University of Minnesota Press, 1960), p. 162.

15. Ibid., p. 167.

16. *Nicomachean Ethics,* Rackham trans., pp. 5-6 (1, n. 4-7, 1094a-b).

17. I.i. 71a, 1-11.

18. I.iii. 1b, 6-1.

19. We should note that we do not follow Richard Weaver's reading of Plato *versus* Aristotle concerning the role of dialectics because, though his argument is correct on Plato, the distinction modifies the role of reasoning within Aristotle's articulation of rhetoric a bit more than makes us comfortable; see *The Ethics of Rhetoric* (Chicago: Henry Regnery, 1953), pp. 3-29.

20. See above, note 12.

21. *Rhetoric,* pp. 31-32.

22. *Rhetoric,* p. 30.

23. *An Examination of the Place of Reason in Ethics* (Cambridge, England: Cambridge University Press, 1950), p. 137.

24. Eric Voegelin, *Anamnesis,* trans. Gerhart Niemeyer (Notre Dame: University of Notre Dame Press, 1978), pp. 206-13.

25. *Federalist,* No. 63.

26. *Ethics of Rhetoric,* p. 83.

27. Ibid., pp. 79-80.

28. *Leadership* (New York: Basic Books, 1978), p. 4.

29. *Scientific Man vs. Power Politics* (Chicago: University of Chicago Press, 1946), p. 10.

Commentary
The Paradox of Rhetoric
KLAUS VONDUNG

Rhetoric has been connected with politics from its beginning as a particular method or "art" of public speech. It is of fundamental interest in the context of our general theme because of the contrasting roles it has played in this connection and because of the controversial interpretations of these roles. On the one hand, rhetoric has been used and understood as a mediator between philosophical knowledge and political action and thus as a means, as Professors Graham and Havard put it, "to translate *sophia* into political *praxis*." On the other hand, rhetoric has been misused for dubious or bad purposes and therefore has been criticized as a dangerous and contemptible technique of deception and seduction. The full range of possibilities and problems that rhetoric presents was realized during the early stages of its development as a particular *techne*. I intend to concentrate on some major points that those early studies and discussions brought to our attention; it is to be hoped that this will also serve as a supplement to George Graham and William Havard's interpretation of Aristotle's concept of rhetoric.

Although there had been public and, in a sense, political speeches before the development of rhetoric, the origin of a system of rules, which defines how to speak well and successfully in public, is a noteworthy occurrence. It is significant that rhetoric originated in connection with a particular historical event: the overthrow of tyranny in three major Sicilian cities between 471 and 461 B.C. The newly established democratic regimes made it possible, and necessary, to discuss and decide political as well as judicial matters in public. It became important to speak convincingly in court and assembly in order to gain majorities. Hence rhetoric developed as a *techne* that could be taught and learned and whose major concern was the genres of the forensic and political speeches. In 427 B.C. rhetoric was brought from Sicily to Athens by Gorgias of Leontinoi. In Athens the introduction of a democratic regime by Cleisthenes (509-507 B.C.) together with further political and juridical reforms by Ephialtes and Pericles (462-458 B.C.) had created, as in Sicily, a favorable climate for the use and success of the new *techne.*[1]

In addition to observing the connection between the origin of rhetoric and the establishment of a democratic and lawful political order, we should note a second point that is important for an adequate evaluation of the possibilities and problems of rhetoric; that is, rhetoric made use, probably from the beginning, of the dialectical method developed by the Eleatic philosophers, mainly Parmenides and Zeno.[2] The close connection between rhetoric and dialectic is confirmed by Aristotle, who begins his treatise on *The "Art" of Rhetoric* with the statement: "Rhetoric is a counterpart of dialectic."[3] In order to understand the consequences of the connection between rhetoric and dialectic, it is useful to recall the major changes the dialectical method underwent from the Eleatic philosophers to Aristotle.

Basically, dialectic is a method to discuss contradictory statements. The general scheme of such a discussion can be gathered from Aristotle's *Topics:* The dialectician presents to his opponent a pair of contradictory statements in the form of a question; the opponent decides that one of the statements is correct. Then the dialectician tries to prove the contrary statement by questioning the opponent in such a way that his answers form the steps of a deductive argumentation that lead to the final conclusion that the opponent's original decision was wrong.[4]

The usefulness of this method for purpose of public speech is clear. In court as well as in political assembly a decision usually has to be made between the arguments of conflicting positions. Although in public speaking one cannot question an opponent, one can translate the steps and points of the two-sided dialectical argumentation into a one-sided rhetorical argument.

If we want to understand the quarrels about rhetoric, especially the conflicting views of Plato and Aristotle, we must recall that at the time of Zeno and Gorgias dialectic was a highly developed, sophisticated method, indifferent to internal content. Originally the dialectical questioning was not necessarily indifferent to the search for truth;[5] later, as a method of formal reasoning, dialectic tended to evolve into a mere instrument, applicable to the proof of any problem or statement, true or false. Finally, it was the pride of a good dialectician (who was then called a *Sophist*) to be able to prove either one of the contradictory statements in a given dialectical question. Consequently, rhetoric, which made use of this method, could serve as a tool for any purpose.

In Plato's time, dialectic and rhetoric were the twin methods dominating intellectual debate and public speech. It is interesting that Plato adopted and reevaluated dialectic and at the same time rejected and depreciated rhetoric. He rejected rhetoric because it was not an *episteme* but a mere instrument, indifferent to the truth of its content, and therefore open to error and deception. In *Gorgias* he stated: "Thus rhetoric, it seems, is a producer of persuasion for belief, not for instruction in the matter of justice and injustice *(peri to dikaion te kai adikon).*"[6] Of course the method of dialectic Plato found in his time was just as indifferent to "the matter of justice and injustice" as rhetoric; if it was more of an "instruction," it was so only in the sense of formal reasoning.

Plato, however, changed the meaning and status of dialectic fundamentally. He adopted the formal method of argumentation but directed it to serve truth. In *Gorgias* he redefined the term *techne: Techne* can give an account of "the real nature *(physis)* of the things it applies," and it can "tell the cause *(aitia)* of any of them."[7] In the light of this definition rhetoric is not even a *techne* but only a "kind of exercise," a "flattery" to please and deceive the soul.[8] Plato's definition of *techne* shows that his own *techne* of dialectic has become an *episteme* as well — that is, the highest possible *episteme,* which gives an account of "the Good" *(agathon)* as the source *(aitia)* of all being and knowlege.[9] Thus dialectic as *episteme* and *techne* is the center of Plato's philosophizing and virtually identical with his understanding of "philosophy."

One might ask why Plato chose the method of dialectic as a framework for his *episteme* in the first place? Could he not have chosen rhetoric instead of dialectic, since in either case he still had to develop the epistemological content, which was necessary to focus the method? Or could he not have built up his *episteme* of the *agathon* independently, on a superior level, in order to master both methods, dialectic as well as rhetoric? If we consider that Aristotle reduced dialectic again to an instrumental method, that at the same time he restored rhetoric as a useful "art," that on the other hand he developed separate *epistemai* of metaphysics, analytics, and ethics, these questions are not so far-fetched and useless as they may seem at first sight; perhaps they open the way to additional insights into the problems of rhetoric. Before we follow this train of thought, it will be useful to recall some aspects of Aristotle's view of rhetoric.

George Graham and William Havard have stated that for Aristotle rhetoric, although "neutral as to internal content," is "an art to be placed in the service of sciences, . . . a means in the service of truth," that it "is treated as an important communicative extension of *noesis*," that it "provides a method of transition from *episteme* to *praxis*," and that as such it is "the means of proper political education of the citizen." Without doubt Aristotle restored rhetoric because it can indeed be useful for a proper political education, if guided by proper standards. Probably it was Aristotle's intention to make rhetoric a kind of link between *sophia*, the source of the standards, and political *praxis*. Nevertheless, he ran into epistemological difficulties, at least partly caused by his inclination to systematize.

Aristotle defined *sophia* as the combination of *nous*, which enables one to grasp the truth about first principles *(archai)*, and of *episteme*, which enables one to draw conclusions from the *archai*. Thus, *episteme* is concerned with necessary and invariable matters, whereas *techne* and *phronesis* relate to *poiesis* and *praxis* as the domains of contingent matters.[10] *Sophia, nous, episteme, techne,* and *phronesis* together form the dianoetical virtues, the virtues of the rational part of the soul.

Although they are connected with each other, since they are ultimately rooted in the divine *nous,* the distinction between invariable and contingent matters makes it difficult to realize the transition from *sophia* or *episteme* to *praxis* when it comes to the question of method. Aristotle carefully distinguished between the methods of *episteme* and those of *phronesis, techne,* and other faculties *(dynameis)* relating to the realm of contingent matters. As to their formal structure, the methods are similar; but as to their validity, they are different. The former, the methods of analytical demonstration, rest on true principles and arrive at true conclusions; the latter, the methods of dialectical and rhetorical argumentation, rest on opinions or probabilities and arrive at conclusions that are only probable. Peter Weber-Schäfer has recently pointed out that by the standards of formal logic, a conclusion pertaining to contingent matters cannot be drawn from true premises, which pertain to the realm of invariable matters.[11] Aristotle himself emphasized the limits of dialectic and rhetoric:

> In proportion as anyone endeavors to make of dialectic or rhetoric, not what they are, faculties *(dynameis),* but sciences *(epistemai),* to that extent he will, without knowing it, destroy their real nature, in thus altering their character, by crossing over into the domain of sciences, whose subjects are certain definite things, not merely words.[12]

Apart from the epistemological dilemma that dialectic and rhetoric cannot serve as methods of *episteme,* there is, in addition, a pedagogical or psychological difficulty that arises from the difference between instruction and persuasion:

> In dealing with certain persons, even if we possessed the most accurate scientific knowledge, we should not find it easy to persuade them by the employment of such knowledge. For scientific discourse is concerned with instruction, but in the case of such persons instruction is impossible; our proofs and arguments must rest on generally accepted principles, as we said in the *Topics,* when speaking of converse with the multitude.[13]

The rhetorical method of argumentation has to operate with examples instead of deduction, and with *enthymemata,* the rhe-

KLAUS VONDUNG

torical equivalent of dialectical deduction, instead of analytical syllogisms. Since this kind of argumentation cannot prove the truth of its conclusions, errors and deceptions cannot be excluded. Aristotle had to admit the possibility of misuse, but in contrast to Plato, he maintained that rhetoric was nonetheless a "good thing":

> If it is argued that one who makes an unfair use of such faculty of speech may do a great deal of harm, this objection applies equally to all good things except virtue, and above all to those things which are most useful, such as strength, health, wealth, generalship; for as these, rightly used, may be of the greatest benefit, so, wrongly used, they may do an equal amount of harm.[14]

But how do we make the right use of rhetoric when there is no methodical guidance through *episteme*? Is it only through goodwill, or even mere chance, that we find the probabilities that come as close to truth as possible in the realm of contingent matters? Yet, as Aristotle explains, the relation between truth and probabilities is much less accidental:

> For, in fact, the true and that which resembles it come under the purview of the same faculty, and at the same time men have a sufficient natural capacity for the truth and indeed in most cases attain to it; wherefore one who divines well in regard to the truth will also be able to divine well in regard to probabilities.[15]

Although there is no epistemological link between truth and the probabilities of rhetorical argumentation, there is an existential link: the soul of man (of the orator as well as his listeners), which is capable of actualizing *all* the dianoetical virtues. It is true that rhetoric can be perverted, but virtue cannot, as Aristotle emphasizes. Because of their virtue, the orator and his listeners will be able to link the rhetorical argument with truth.[16]

Thus Aristotle tried to overcome the ethical indifference of rhetoric by placing it under the reign of virtue. Although Plato had rejected rhetoric, he nonetheless had established the foundation on which Aristotle could construct the philosophical connection between truth and rhetoric. Aristotle's argument

98

that "the true and that which resembles it come under the purview of the same faculty" and that "one who divines well in regard to the truth will also be able to divine well in regard to probabilities" refers directly to Socrates' statement in *Phaedrus* "that the multitude get their notion of probability as the result of a likeness to truth . . . [and] that these likenesses can always be best discovered by one who knows the truth."[17]

Why, then, had Plato not drawn the same conclusion as Aristotle, making use of rhetoric, under these premises, as a means of political education instead of rejecting it? We return to the questions raised before. To begin with, Plato's rejection of rhetoric was not so radical as the harsh condemnation in *Gorgias* suggests. In *Phaedrus* we find a more differentiated, though rather confusing, evaluation of rhetoric. On the one hand, Plato repeats his general disapproval of rhetoric, and on the other hand he concedes "that there is nothing shameful in the mere writing of speeches."[18] Obviously, there can be "good writing and bad," so Plato asks: "What is the nature of good writing?"[19] And he replies that "a good and successful discourse presupposes a knowledge in the mind of the speaker of the truth about his subject."[20] It seems as though Plato could come to the same conclusion as Aristotle, derived from the likeness between truth and probability. But this is not quite the case.

The basic subject of any speech, Plato says, not only of the particular genres of forensic and political speeches, is the soul, because in the soul we actualize the love for the Good, which is the source of all being and knowledge, and because "it is there that the speaker is attempting to implant conviction."[21] Yet the truth about the soul (and with it the truth about all other matters) can be grasped only in the *episteme* of dialectic and by means of "scientific discourse."[22] Does Plato thus revoke his concession that speeches (i.e., written, public, and thus rhetorical speeches) also can be good? Plato's final conclusion seems to be paradoxical:

> The conditions to be fulfilled are these: first, you must know the truth about the subject that you *speak or write* about: that is to say, you must be able to isolate it in definition and having

so defined it you must next understand how to divide it into kinds, until you reach the limit of division; secondly, you must have a corresponding discernment of the nature of the soul, discover the type of speech appropriate to each nature, and order and arrange your discourse accordingly, addressing a variegated soul in a variegated style that ranges over the whole gamut of tones, and a simple soul in a simple style. All this must be done if you are to become competent, within human limits, as a scientific practitioner of speech, whether you propose to instruct or to persuade.[23]

It is obvious that these conditions cannot be fulfilled in a public speech where one has to address a multitude of people whose different souls one does not know. An additional obstacle is the character of rhetorical speech as a necessarily written genre. (Only in writing can a speech be arranged as perfectly as the "art" of rhetoric demands, and because of its artistic construction, it has to be fixed in writing, otherwise one could not learn and remember it by heart, which is essential for its authentic presentation in court or assembly or elsewhere—Lysias's speech in the beginning of *Phaedrus* exemplifies this.) Writing as such is an obstacle to truth, as Plato contends:

Anyone who leaves behind him a written manual, and likewise anyone who takes it over from him, on the supposition that such writing will provide something reliable and permanent, must be exceedingly simple-minded.[24]

And he continues that

a written discourse on any subject necessarily contains a good deal of play, and that no such discourse, whether in verse or prose, deserves to be treated too seriously, but that the best of them were composed only as means of reminding those who know the truth.[25]

Plato's general depreciation of writing aggravates the paradox of the possibility of conveying truth in speech because it includes even his own dialogues, which are fictitious and written literature. If we cannot solve this paradox, we can at least try to get one step further in its interpretation by examining the form of writing in which the paradox is expressed.

The dialogue *Phaedrus* is carefully structured in a succession of ascending steps. It begins with Lysias's speech on love, which serves as an example for a bad speech: It does not define the nature of love and therefore draws wrong conclusions, and it is badly composed. Then follows Socrates' first speech, which is better conceived insofar as it gives a reasonable definition of love, draws more logical conclusions, and is structured more skillfully. But, as a mere antithesis to Lysias's speech, it still clings too much to this bad example and is better only in terms of formal reasoning and composition. Hence, Socrates starts afresh and in a second speech unfolds the true nature of love as a divine force connecting our soul with the true Being. He tells the truth about love, the soul, and the true Being, using a myth, because the telling of a story agrees particularly well with the closed form of the speech and the telling also meets the rhetorical principle of convincing by examples. Yet, for the very reason that the truth was told in a myth, a further step has to be made: When Socrates has finished his second speech he enters into a dialogue with Phaedrus, which not only allows him to reiterate and differentiate in dialectical discourse what he said before but also enables him to discuss the methods one uses to speak about truth, that is, to make the mode of speaking itself the subject of the discourse. And now Socrates comes forth with the surprising statement that everything written, be it speech or discourse, cannot offer "true wisdom, but only its semblance."[26]

Since the preceding sequence of speeches and dialogue represents ascending modes of transmitting truth, it is in the logic of the sequence that Socrates' statement points to a further step. Indeed, Plato takes an ultimate step that reaches beyond the dialogue *Phaedrus* itself, for this dialogue is after all a piece of written literature. The mode of speaking that comes closest to the truth is "the living discourse, the original of which the written discourse may fairly be called a kind of image,"[27] because

clearness and perfection and serious value are only in those spoken discourses that are set forth for the sake of instruction, and are veritably written in the soul of the listener, and have the Just *(dikaion)* and the Beautiful *(kalon)* and the Good *(agathon)* for subjects.[28]

The living discourse is by far superior to the written one because only there is the dialectician able to employ the art of dialectic in its full meaning, that is,

> to select a soul of the right type, and in it plant and sow his words founded on knowledge, words which can defend both themselves and him who planted them, words which instead of remaining barren contain a seed whence new words grow up in new characters; whereby the seed is vouchsafed immortality, and its possessor the fullest measure of blessedness that man can attain unto.[29]

Now we can answer the question why Plato chose dialectic as the methodical framework of his philosohy: Plato understood the dialectical dialogue not as a mere method of argumentation but as the existential event in which truth unfolds itself in words through the loving interchange of souls that love the truth and jointly search for it.

Nevertheless, we can conclude that the final statements of Plato in *Phaedrus* do not entirely revoke his concession that good rhetorical speech is possible, nor do they invalidate his actual speech about the true nature of love or the dialogue *Phaedrus* itself. Although Plato did not solve the paradox of speaking and writing about truth, he attentuated it, or rather developed an additional view on a different level, by interpreting written speech not as the contradiction but as the "brother" of living discourse,[30] and by placing the different kinds of speeches and dialogue into a sequence in which they represent ascending modes of conveying truth.

With respect to the question of how Plato's final judgment on rhetoric has to be understood, it is noteworthy that the speech of Socrates on the true nature of love forms the structural center of *Phaedrus*. This speech is declared an "exquisite game of the man who is able to play with speech by telling myths about justice and other matters," in contrast to the "vile game" Lysias's speech represented, but also in contrast to the "serious treatment" of truth in the living dialectical discourse.[31] The written dialectical discourse, as we find it in *Phaedrus,* stands between the mythical story and the living discourse; it participates in both: in the truth unfolded in living discourse, but also in the rhetorical character of speech; and it combines, in the very form in which Plato designed his dialogues, the "seriousness" of conversing about truth and the "play" of inventing myths and composing works of literature.[32]

One might conclude that Plato's final judgment on rhetoric was twofold. On the one hand, the hierarchy of speeches and dialogue, which he established, as well as the fact that he wrote speeches himself and used rhetorical elements in his dialogues, allow the conclusion that rhetorical speech can also participate in the truth as the living discourse unfolds, though only as its lesser brother. This conclusion would be similar to Aristotle's view. On the other hand, Plato strictly maintained that for the search and mediation of truth, rhetoric was an inadequate instrument. Thus the paradox remains, and the task remains for us to make the right use of rhetoric in view of this paradox.

Notes

1. Cf. Cicero *Brutus* 12.46; Gerd Ueding, *Einführung in die Rhetorik* (Stuttgart: Metzler, 1976), pp. 14-15; Tuttu Tarkiainen, *Die athenische Demokratie* (Zürich: Artemis, 1966), pp. 124-25.
2. Cf. Giorgio Colli, *Die Geburt der Philosophie* (Frankfurt: Europäische Verlagsanstalt, 1981), pp. 68-69.
3. Aristotle, *The "Art" of Rhetoric,* trans. J.H. Freese (London: Heinemann, 1926), 1354A.
4. Aristotle *Topics* 104, 108; cf. Colli, *Die Geburt der Philosophie,* pp. 69-71.
5. Cf. Colli, *Die Geburt der Philosophie,* pp. 69, 72.
6. Plato, *Gorgias,* trans. W.R.M. Lamb (London: Heinemann, 1925), 455A.
7. Ibid., 465A.
8. Ibid., 462B-465E.
9. Cf. Plato *Republic* bk. 4.
10. Cf. Aristotle *Nicomachean Ethics* bk. 6.
11. Peter Weber-Schäfer, "Politik und die Kunst der Überzeugung," in *The Philosophy of Order: Festschrift for Eric Voegelin,* ed. P.J. Opitz and G. Sebba (Stuttgart: Klett-Cotta, 1981), pp. 345-58.
12. Aristotle *Rhetoric* 1359B.

13. Ibid., 1355A.
14. Ibid., 1355B.
15. Ibid., 1355A.
16. Cf. Weber-Schäfer, "Politik und die Kunst der Überzeugung," pp. 356-57.
17. Plato, *Phaedrus,* trans. R. Hackforth (Cambridge, England: Cambridge University Press, 1972), 273D.
18. Ibid., 258D. Plato always and only uses the noun *logos,* or the verb *legein,* for the different types of rhetorical "speech" vs. scientific or dialectical "discourse," written "speech" vs. "living discourse" (i.e., spoken dialectical dialogue); the differing English translations depend on the context in which the Greek terms appear.
19. Ibid.
20. Ibid., 259E.
21. Ibid., 271A; cf. 246D-248B.
22. Ibid., 270E, 271D-272B.
23. Ibid., 277B.
24. Ibid., 275C.
25. Ibid., 277E-278A.
26. Ibid., 275A.
27. Ibid., 276A.
28. Ibid., 278A.
29. Ibid., 276E-277A.
30. Ibid., 276A.
31. Ibid., 276E.
32. Cf. the similar paradox of "seriousness" and "play" in *Republic* 545D-546A.

THOMAS E. FLANAGAN

Hayek's Concept of Constructivism 4

Friedrich Hayek began his academic career with studies in economics at the University of Vienna where one of his most famous teachers was Ludwig Von Mises. Hayek quickly went on to establish himself as a foremost theoretical economist of the day, concentrating on such fields as the business cycle, money, prices, and the debate over planning. Since the 1940s, however, he has published very little technical economics, and the announcement of the Nobel Prize in Economic Science, which he won in 1974, states that he was being honored not only for work in economics but also for "penetrating analysis of the interdependence of economic, social and institutional phenomena."[1]

His best-known book of political theory is still *The Road to Serfdom* (1944), which argued that totalitarianism, whether of the left or right, is the logical outcome of central planning. Republished as a *Reader's Digest* condensed book, *The Road to Serfdom* was read by millions and is a classic of modern liberalism. However, it is no longer an adequate guide to Hayek's thinking, which has developed considerably in the intervening years. Hayek's magnum opus is *Law, Legislation and Liberty* (1973-79), whose three volumes must be considered the definitive expression of his thought. This essay is based chiefly on *Law, Legislation and Liberty* with references as necessary to other works such as *The Counter-Revolution of Science* (1955), *The Constitution of Liberty* (1960), three volumes of collected essays, and numerous pamphlets and occasional papers.[2]

Apart from polemical attacks like Herman Finer's *Road to Reaction,* the secondary literature on Hayek is surprisingly small. A good book of essays dealing with the *Constitution of Liberty* was published in 1961, and another collection appeared in 1976.[3] One recent book has tried to assess Hayek's importance as an economist; another book, by Norman P. Barry, explores the wider dimensions of his thought as well as his contribution to economics.[4] Barry's work is largely expository and confines criticism to pointing out certain inconsistencies or antinomies in Hayek's thinking. A searching analysis of his philosophy has yet to be written, and it will not be easily accomplished, for his work ranges so widely over economics, philosophy, methodology, psychology, history, politics, and jurisprudence that few critics can evaluate all his ideas. Yet the job must be done if Barry is correct that "Hayek's complete works form one of the most profound political philosophies written this century."[5] I would agree with Barry's assessment as long as the accent is on "political" rather than "philosophy." Hayek's work is a searching investigation of the relation between state and society. He has a great deal to teach us about the "agenda" and "nonagenda" of government, to use Bentham's phrase; and he has an interesting perspective on ethical questions seen from a utilitarian point of view. But he has little to say about the deeper questions of the meaning and destiny of human existence. Without at all denigrating its importance, one can say that Hayek's work is only a part of the philosophic enterprise as originally conceived.

This essay is not so ambitious as to attempt a complete analysis of Hayek's thought. It presents a single concept, "constructivism," which is particularly relevant to the themes of politics, *sophia* and *praxis*.

Order Versus Organization[6]

Hayek distinguishes two fundamentally different kinds of social structure.[7] One, which he calls "organization," "made order," or *taxis,* is a deliberate arrangement of elements according to the conscious intention of some person or group, expressed in the form of commands and subsidiary rules. Examples of organizations are business firms, government agencies, churches, and voluntary associations or, at a different level, legal structures like the Criminal Code or artificial languages like Esperanto. All have been deliberately created to serve some conscious human purpose.

The second kind of structure, called "self-generating order," "spontaneous order," "grown order," or *cosmos,* emerges from the mutual interaction of elements. It is not imposed by command nor created by design. It is the "result of human action but not the execution of any human design," to cite a phrase of Adam Ferguson that Hayek often quotes.[8] A perfect example of spontaneous order is human language. No single intelligence has created our languages; they are products of evolutionary growth from beginnings that are now only conjectural. Other self-generating orders are the marketplace, studied by economics, human population dynamics, and demography. One could also mention the common law, which is certainly structured but is not superintended by any single authority, as well as the "republic of science," whose principles of order were sketched out in a famous essay by Michael Polanyi.[9] Society itself is an all-inclusive spontaneous order, composed of subordinate organizations and orders that mutually adjust to one another.

Order and organization should be understood as ideal types found together in concrete social phenomena. A university, for example, is formally an organization with an administrative hierarchy culminating in a president and board of directors. Yet the reality is more complex, for a large university consists of a multitude of semiautonomous units competing with one another for students, research funds, and other resources. Official decisions often result more from a balance of conflicting forces than from a fiat by the administration. Concepts of order and organization are tools to analyze situations, not mere labels to be pinned on social structures.

Both kinds of structure depend upon man's propensity to follow rulers. Indeed, the essence of a human order, system, or structure is that behavior limited by rules produces patterns of intelligibility, regularity, and predictability. But the rules are different in the two cases. An organization depends upon commands that are consciously given and consciously obeyed. The epitome of the made order is its rulebook, administrative manual, or bylaws. In contrast, a spontaneous order demands only that individuals follow rules, not that they be able to state them or even be aware of them. To use a distinction well known to philosophers, individuals within a self-generating order need to "know that" certain conduct is required; they need not "know what" are the rules they follow.

Hayek uses the Greek word *thesis* to describe the rules of an organization. *Thesis* is defined as "any rule which is applicable only to particular people or in the service of the ends of rulers." In contrast, a rule of a spontaneous order is called *nomos,* defined as "a universal rule of just conduct applying to an unknown number of future instances and equally to all persons in the objective circumstances described by the rule, irrespective of the effects which observance of the rule will produce in a particular situation."[10]

Nomoi allow an overall order to emerge that no one designed, intended, or foresaw. This is what Adam Smith meant to say for the special case of the market with his famous metaphor of the "invisible hand." In seeking their self-interest under certain rules of honesty, justice, and respect for agreements, men create an order in which the pursuit of private gain leads them to serve the interests of others. As supply and demand equilibrate, resources are optimally allocated to participants. The slightly occult term "invisible hand" appropriately expresses our amazement at a process that is miraculous in the sense that we could never consciously design an equally efficient way of accomplishing the same goal.

The rules of spontaneous orders such as language, common law, and the market have themselves evolved spontaneously, a point on which Hayek lays great stress; he wishes to emphasize that the undirected process of social evolution yields results far superior to what human intellect could consciously devise. But he also holds that as men gradually begin to understand these rules through philosophy and social science, it becomes possible to think of improving them through deliberate alteration and experimentation.[11] Such improvement is possible as long as it is done in harmony with the immanent principles of an order and not to replace them. Commentators have noted that Hayek has not made it entirely clear how men, who move within an order they can never wholly comprehend, can hope to improve it through intentional design.[12] This is one of several tensions in his thought that arise from his unique combination of liberal rationalism and the conservatism of Edmund Burke.

The word "spontaneous" does not mean there is no need for coercive enforcement of the rules of order. Language may not need enforcement, but common law and the market certainly do. It is often in our short-term interest to violate rules on the assumption that others will obey them, thus giving us a special advantage. For example, most thieves do not want to abolish the institution of private property, they just want to appropriate the property of others. In the jargon of contemporary economics, they are "free riders." Enforcement against free riders is acceptable and indeed essential to many spontaneous orders.

There are three major differences beween spontaneous and made orders which can be tabulated as follows:[13]

	Organization	*Spontaneous Order*
tends to	simplicity	complexity
tends to	concreteness	abstractness
serves	purpose of the maker	no single purpose

Organization tends to simple structures, divisions, and hierarchies because it is a product of the limited powers of one or a few conscious minds. But since spontaneous order is not bound by the need of a superintending intelligence, it can become as complex as circumstances demand. Bertrand de Jouvenel has clearly illustrated this point with his "problem of the orchard."[14] Tell a group of schoolboys that a hundred thousand apples are to be harvested, and ask how they should be piled. The answer will usually be a thousand piles of a hundred apples or a hundred piles of a thousand, symmetrically spaced throughout the orchard. Now ask the boys to actually harvest and heap up the apples, without direct supervision. A complex and unsymmetrical assortment of heaps will result, reflecting the skills, strength, and industry of the different pickers, as well as peculiarities of the individual trees. This complex order may offend the rationalistic mind, but the apples will have been harvested more efficiently than if a predetermined plan had been imposed.

Organizations also tend to concreteness, which is to say that particular people are put in particular places and told to do specified things. "Go to this office, do this job, file this report, hire this person." But a spontaneous order is abstract in that the positions of individuals are not specified. A market demands buyers and sellers, but it does not matter who nor how many play these roles. This again is an advantage of order over organization. If individuals are free to play their own roles, assuming they abide by necessary general rules, they are better able to use knowledge that only they possess.

Abstractness is a matter of degree. Hayek interprets human progress as an increase in the abstractness of social relations. Rules of conduct become less specific in the obligations they impose on men. Obligations of fair dealing are generalized from family, relatives, and friends to apply to all with whom one comes in contact. Hayek uses the terms Great Society and Open Society, borrowed from Adam Smith and Karl Popper respectively, to denote the highly abstract Western society of recent centuries.[15]

Finally, an organization serves the purpose of its makers. Government enforces the law, a corporation makes money, and a church unites people to worship. More than one purpose might be pursued (governments also deliver mail and pave roads), but this does not affect the principle that purpose is consciously imposed from above. A spontaneous order, in comparison, cannot be said to have a purpose. It is a milieu or matrix that helps individuals to pursue their own goals in infinite profusion. It provides means but not ends, as is clearly true of language, common law, or the market. Society as a whole, which is a spontaneous order, has no purpose beyond facilitating the various ends of its participants. Like Jouvenel, Hayek insists that the only intelligible meaning of the term "common good" for society as a whole is the maintenance of a system of rules which makes human action possible.[16] The Great Society is one in which agreement is obtained about the means of action in order to allow men greater access to ends of their own choosing.[17]

At this point one must acknowledge a gap in Hayek's otherwise logical treatment. His Great Society is a purely abstract concept denoting the totality of human transactions and the web of interrelationships. It is not a concrete community bounded in space and time. Men live in the means-connected order of the Great Society, but they also live in ends-connected communities that give purpose to their lives. These communities are bound together by specific emotional ties: friendship *(philia)* in the *polis,* dynastic loyalty in the empire, nationalism in the nation-state.

A simple argument will show that these communities are essential to keep the Great Society in being. If other humans are only means to my ends, what incentive do I have to abide by the rules of conduct that make the Great Society functional? I am always tempted to be an ethical "free rider," lying, cheating, or stealing to promote my own interests. To constrain a society of purely self-interested individuals who regard each other only as means, there would have to be such a powerful coercive apparatus of rule enforcement that Hayek's liberalism would be destroyed. Only if men share a mutual sympathy based on common purpose can they be counted on to refrain from plundering each other. Or in other words, community is necessary to the Great Society. This argument could be integrated into Hayek's thought without disturbing the larger structure of ideas, but his work as it stands has not taken sufficient account of the problem. He tends to dismiss as "tribalism" emotional experiences like nationalism that are the substance of community.[18]

Neither order nor organization is intrinsically superior to the other; each is useful to mankind, and each has its special strength. Organization is particularly efficient where one purpose is to be pursued to the exclusion of others. But the deficiency of organization is that it must be designed, and so can only receive the benefit of a limited amount of intelligence. Spontaneous order, on the other hand, allows for the continuing contribution of many minds over time. Thus arise structures like language, which no one could ever have created or even envisioned.

This last point is particularly important because all intelligences are severely limited in one crucial way. Even the most brilliant mind has little knowledge of the particular circumstances of others' lives.[19] An architect may know much about house building, but he knows little of the particular needs, desires, and financial resources of those who want homes. A spontaneous order allows these quanta of particular knowledge to be adjusted to one another. The very fact that spontaneous order is unplanned and undesigned makes it superior to organization in using the plenitude of information that is available in the separated minds of men.

Society as a whole is a spontaneous order, though many organizations act within it. The remarkable progress of civilization, particularly of the West in modern times, bears testimony to the power of spontaneous order. The absence of imposed purpose allows free play to creative initiative while maintaining an effective filtering system to sort out beneficial innovations. Ego proposes, but Other disposes. The individual's freedom to initiate is matched by others' freedom to reject, accept, or imitate. In this way words are coined, ideas accepted, marriages concluded, and commodities sold.

Also, spontaneous order itself is always changing because its rules are modified through the pressure of initiative and acceptance. There is an evolutionary process of "survival of the fittest"—not of men, but of rules.[20] Those groups that follow rules of, say, kinship or property that strengthen them will prevail over groups whose innovations are less constructive. Historical progress is not an accident but a logical result of the power of spontaneous order to solve by experimentation problems that overmatch the power of human intellects taken singly.

This progress, however, increases man's power to understand and organize his affairs. Thus consciously designed social structures play an ever more prominent part in our lives. Large corporations provide goods and services that smaller entrepreneurs could not offer. Legislation regularizes and partially replaces common law. Books of grammar help standardize linguistic usage, making a language understood over a larger area and retarding its spontaneous division into mutually unintelligible dialects. It is often assumed from observation of such developments that man is now able to take control of his own affairs. Hayek draws precisely the opposite conclusion. Progress enhances the complexity of the Great Society, rendering it ever harder to plan as a whole. Organized structures within it are still vitally dependent on spontaneous evolution. Corporate planning would be irrational without the objective data of prices furnished by the market. It is commonplace to political scientists that legislation creates as many problems as it solves, problems that can be resolved only through the adjudication of cases in which a new structure of interpretation gradually arises. And a language whose grammar never changed would be a dead language, not a living vehicle of communication.

Constructivism

What Hayek now calls "constructivism" is not a new concept in his philosophy. In *The Constitution of Liberty* he called it "rationalism" *tout court;* to this false rationalism he opposed the true position of "evolutionary rationalism" or "antirationalism."[21] But this terminology was confusing and bound to lead to misunderstanding. Hence in 1964 he introduced the term "constructivism."[22] He expanded on it at length in 1970 in his inaugural lecture at the University of Salzburg,[23] and he used it consistently in *Law, Legislation and Liberty.*

Constructivism is the intellectual error of interpreting order as if it were organization, that is, of assuming that self-generating structures must be deliberately made and controlled by man. The logical conclusion from this erroneous premise is that "since

man had himself created the institutions of society and civilization, he must also be able to alter them at will so as to satisfy
his desires or wishes."[24] Constructivism flatters man by making him appear the master of his fate, occupying the creative
role that Judaeo-Christian belief reserves for God.

Constructivism involves the "synoptic delusion," the "fiction
that all the relevant facts are known to some one mind and that
it is possible to construct from this knowledge of the particulars
a desirable social order."[25] The fallacy is evident in the light
of Hayek's position. Order is man's evolutionary response to
the ineluctable ignorance of the individual mind. It is a way
of knitting together separate intelligences so that each may contribute information known only to itself. Order exists precisely in situations where no single mind can take a synoptic view.

Constructivism is as mistaken about rules as it is about
order. Hayek points out that there are three levels of rules of
human conduct: (1) those we follow without being able to state
(a child can speak without knowing a single rule of grammar);
(2) those we have learned to state after having followed in practice (grammar was formulated by the classical grammarians after
thousands of years of language); (3) those consciously laid down
by man (the government of Quebec has created numerous rules
about the use of language in business and public affairs). The
constructivist tends to ignore the rules of the first two kinds
and to see the third as the paradigm of all rules. Tacit rules
are ignored or misinterpreted as the result of conscious creation.[26]

Constructivism often appears in mythopoetic thought. The
myths of archaic man usually explain human institutions as
the gift of the gods. Prometheus brings fire to man in Greek
mythology, and Moses receives the Law directly from God. Such
thinking, from Hayek's point of view, shows an inability to understand how social institutions can emerge from undirected
evolution. The mythopoetic thinker realizes that the men of
his acquaintance could never have created law, language, money,
or other important institutions; but he is unable to think in
terms of emergence rather than creation, and so he attributes
these institutions to the making of the gods.

This may be intellectually naive, but at least it is humble. Cosmogonic myths express man's awe and respect for a cosmic order that he knows he has not made. Modern constructivism is a regression to the intellectual naiveté of early man coupled with an arrogant attribution by man to himself of godlike creative power. It is hubris in the strongest sense.

For Hayek, the *fons et origo* of modern constructivism is René Descartes, who paid little attention to social and political questions, but who

> taught that we should only believe what we can prove. Applied to the field of morals and values generally, his doctrine meant that we should only accept as binding what we could recognize as a rational design for a recognizable purpose.[27]

Seventeenth-century political philosophers like Hobbes and Spinoza, both powerfully influenced by Descartes, began to develop the potential of constructivism. Spinoza's *Ethics* was an attempt to elaborate moral science *more geometrico,* as a system deduced from self-evident axioms. Hobbes' famous theory of contract interpreted society as a construct of deliberate agreement, not as an evolutionary formation, while law became nothing more than the will of the sovereign. Hobbes' system was the first comprehensive constructivist theory and is still a model of its kind.

Hayek applies the label "constructivist" to many different tendencies in the social and political thought of recent centuries. Here we can mention only some of the more obvious applications. The "act-utilitarianism" of Bentham is clearly a case in point because it calls on man to judge the morality of actions by assessing whether their consequences contribute to human happiness. This, according to Hayek, is a judgment that we never have enough information to make. The "rule-utilitarianism" of Hume, in contrast, is not constructivist because it makes allowances for the limitations of our knowledge. We must abide by rules precisely because we can never know enough to be good consequentialists.[28]

The legal positivism of Bentham, Austin, and Kelsen is equally an example of constructivism. To construe all valid law as the command of the sovereign is to confuse order, whose rules develop organically, with organization, which does indeed depend upon a structure of proclaimed rules. If pursued to its logical conclusions, legal positivism subsumes the *cosmos* of society into the *taxis* of the state.[29]

What positivism is to the legal sphere, socialism is to the economic sphere. The former decries the barbarous confusion of common law, the latter condemns the "anarchy of the market." The socialist dream is to replace the impersonal process of the market with a centrally planned and controlled organization. This is true of Marxian socialism as well as of the positivism of the Saint-Simonians and of Auguste Comte, in which the whole of society would be ruled by a scientific priesthood and a corporate technocracy.[30]

Finally, even many reformist liberals who eschew central planning or other sweeping visions of social change still think in constructivist terms. The typical "liberal" today believes himself to be a pragmatist who can use the state as needed to remedy "market failures." He is an interventionist rather than a full-fledged socialist. Hayek cogently argues that interventionism is, if anything, a greater fallacy than full-scale socialism. The market is a system whose rules of conduct must be followed because of their general benefit, even if in particular cases the outcome is not one we like. We are not at liberty to accept market outcomes when we approve of them and intervene when we do not. The unintended consequences of such pragmatic interventions will more than outweigh whatever specific good is achieved, as illustrated by the notorious example of rent controls.[31] When partial plans are coercively imposed on the market, they will always engender unwanted results to the extent that participants in the social order retain any freedom to react to governmental fiat. Thus rent controls tend to create a shortage of rental accommodation as private investment capital flows to other areas of the market where higher returns are attainable.

Hayek has done a particularly thorough job of showing the constructivist aspect of the contemporary obsession with "social justice." Advocates of social justice wish to use state power to "redistribute" wealth and income on the basis of merit, desert, or need. But the original distribution that arose from market processes was not a decision of anyone's will; it was the impersonal result of transactions within a self-generating order. "Redistribution" is a deliberate share-out that makes sense only within the context of an organization, a point implied in Aristotle's original conception of distributive justice.[32]

Modern proponents of social justice, having erased the distinction between order and organization, logically enough have conflated commutative and distributive justice into a bastard conception of social justice. Their aims could be achieved only if society were converted from an order into an organization. Then it would become possible to deliberately determine everyone's place in life not on the economic basis of "value" (what others are willing to exchange for one's contribution) but on the political criteria of merit, desert, or need (what others think of one as a person). Hayek's critique of social justice effectively explodes one of the most prevalent superstitions of our age.[33]

The *Road to Serfdom* made Hayek famous by arguing that state planning implies totalitarianism. The argument was that planning would inevitably lead to state controls on employment, residence, mobility, and other fundamental freedoms. It was not meant as an empirical prediction that so many years of a socialist government would produce totalitarianism. It was instead an analytical proposition that the internal logic of planning eventuates in totalitarianism.[34]

Hayek now holds the same view of constructivism generally. Socialism, positivism, et al. become totalitarian if they are followed consistently. The result is implied in the desire to transform society from an order into an organization. If this is indeed possible, it can be achieved only by submitting all aspects of social life to the coercive control of the state. Society must be remade, by force if necessary, to fit the rationally designed scheme. From Hayek's point of view, this attempt, though it pretends to be the implementation of a rational plan, is the height of unreason. It deliberately rejects the proven ability of spontaneous order to solve problems that transcend individual reason, in favour of the limited knowledge that must constrain any organization. One is reminded of the famous saying of Montesquieu about despotism: "Quand les sauvages de la Louisiane veulent avoir du fruit, ils coupent l'arbre au pied, et cueillent le fruit. Voilà le gouvernement despotique."[35] Rational statesmanship is the cultivation of society, the enforcement and patient improvement of the rules of conduct upon which spontaneous order rests. Constructivism is the irrational application of will, in disregard of the immanent principles of order. It could be called a regression to barbarism, except that would be unfair to our ancestors. It is rather a self-destructive temptation of reason that is too proud to acknowledge its limits. The essence of the matter was formulated with breathtaking arrogance by Mao Tse-tung at the time of the Great Leap Forward (1958):

> Apart from their other characteristics, China's 600 million people have two remarkable peculiarities; they are, first of all, poor, and secondly, blank. . . . A clean sheet of paper has no blotches, and so the newest and most beautiful pictures can be painted on it.[36]

Was there ever a more dreadful image of government than to picture society as a *tabula rasa* awaiting the artistic inspiration of the ruler?

Hayek's concept of constructivism is broadly applicable to the ideologies of the modern era. It points to a common tendency, present among them all in varying degree: the desire to submit society to conscious human control through the agency of the state, and a glorification of the knowledge that will allegedly allow society to be remade. Hayek's constructivism would seem to cover about the same territory as Eric Voegelin's concept of Gnosticism,[37] but with a different emphasis. Hayek stresses the remaking of society, whereas Voegelin emphasizes the rebellion of man against transcendent order. Both concepts agree in the importance of *gnosis,* the new knowledge that elevates man above his previous status to become lawgiver to himself. Although Hayek and Voegelin have analyzed the age of ideology from different directions, they have reached very similar conclusions.

Sophia and Praxis

Several worthwhile links can be made between constructivism and the themes of politics, *sophia* and *praxis*. *Sophia* is the virtue of wisdom. One dimension of it was eloquently expressed by Socrates in the *Apology* when he explained the meaning of the Delphic utterance that no one was wiser than he himself. The explanation is that wisdom in a complete sense can be possessed only by God; human wisdom is essentially partial and limited, and largely negative. That is, Socrates is the wisest man on earth because he is conscious of his own ignorance and because he questions the alleged wisdom of others.[38] Philosophy, the "love of wisdom," is a way of life based on questioning. Unlike the hubristic claim of the Hegelian dialectic to be ready to move from the love of knowledge *(Liebe zum Wissen)* to the possession of actual knowledge *(wirkliches Wissen),*[39] the Socratic dialectic leads to more questions than answers.

Hayek's view of human knowledge is quite compatible with this conception of wisdom. The limitation of knowledge is the central theme of his philosophy, from which all else follows, including the critique of constructivism. Socratic and Hayekian philosophy are both doctrines of humility.

However, this is only the first stage of the problem. Although Plato makes Socrates emphasize ignorance in the *Apology,* that is not the whole story of philosophy. Wisdom is the virtue that is the perfection of the rational part of the soul, the *nous.* How it is attained is shown in the parable of the cave. By stages, the philosopher ascends the path of contemplation of order, as manifest in the material world, to contemplation of the immaterial forms, and finally to contemplation of the ultimate source of order.

Aristotle's *Metaphysics* contains essentially the same view of wisdom. Philosophy begins with wonder at the order of the universe and an awareness of our ignorance of causes. As reason seeks an explanation in first principles, it becomes aware that only God could be completely wise. Philosophy is a "divine science" to the extent that it participates in the wisdom of God.[40]

At the highest level, *sophia* is based on *theoria*. This word is inadequately translated as "theory" or as "contemplation" alone; both dimensions are implied.[41] In modern discourse, "theory" means a set of logically interrelated propositions that explains some aspect of the physical or social universe, whereas "contemplation" implies a meditative experience, usually with the connotations of transcendence. The Aristotelian *theoria* combines both meanings because the philosopher achieves the contemplation of the transcendent source of order through a theoretical understanding of the *cosmos*. Platonic-Aristotelian philosophy is, in modern terms, scientific and religious as well as philosophical.

At this point, Hayek parts company with the founders of philosophy. For him, "theory" has no religious dimension. It is contemplation of the order of the universe, the source of which he never discusses, for he understands order as self-generating through an evolutionary process, in the natural world (which we have not had a chance to discuss) as well as in the social. Apart from this, the mood of Hayekian philosophy is not unlike that of classical philosophy, as suggested by his revival of Greek terminology. Man seeks to discover the order of the *cosmos,* which he has not made and which does not depend on his will or conscious decision. It is a reality that objectively transcends the individual person. A close study of Hayek evokes in the student certain experiences akin to those of Greek philosophy. There is, first, humility, as one tries to understand order that human intellect could not consciously create. There is also awe or wonder at the complexity and subtlety of order, for example at the way in which populations equilibrate or the market is cleared. There is a sense of mystery about these processes that depend on *nomos*. According to legend, Plato called for music to be played on the day of his death and indicated the *nomos* of the tune with his finger.[42] Hayekian philosophy engenders the same attitude toward order, which could even be understood as a love of *cosmos*. The reality of spontaneous order, which so far outstrips individual human ability to comprehend it, is irresistibly attractive to one who has come to understand it even imperfectly.

Although Hayek is silent about any religious dimension of wisdom, his philosophy does not run counter to a sense of the divine, and indeed could be a path leading to it. He himself has written: "That we ought not to believe anything which has been shown to be false does not mean that we ought to believe only what has been demonstrated to be true."[43] His refutation of scientism as a species of constructivism leaves the door open for the experience of faith, even if he has said nothing about it.

However, Hayek's philosophy would be incompatible with a theological view of God as personal creator or the Greek view of God as the source of order or as the unmoved mover. Hayek interprets order not as initially given but as emerging over time. To hypostasize order at the beginning of time is a form of naive constructivism, which assumes order must have been designed, if not by the mind of man, then by the mind of God. The greater miracle is that order emerges without design. If there is a Hayekian God, He must be more omega than alpha; or to be more precise, He is like the process by which omega emerges from alpha.

Hayek's philosophy is also relevant to the concept of *praxis,* or action. In the first place, it furnishes an effective critique of one modern concept of *praxis,* which seems to have arisen with August Cieszkowski and to have passed from him to Moses Hess and ultimately to Karl Marx.[44] Cieszkowski's *Prolegomena zur Historiosophie* (1838) drew certain rather plausible conclusions from Hegel's claim to have transformed philosophy from the love of wisdom to the possession of wisdom. Cieszkowski argued that knowledge had run ahead of social reality, that it was now necessary to remake society according to Hegel's Absolute Knowledge. Mankind was about to enter the third and final age of history, characterized by "post-theoretical praxis."[45] The claim to base *praxis* on certainty of knowledge is Cieszkowski's particular contribution, which is expressed in his neologism *Historiosophie.* He explained his programme thus:

> If we might say that from Pythagoras to Hegel we had only *philosophia* whereas with Hegel we attained *sophia,* in a methodologically analogous fashion we could say that here we have treated the passage from a philosophy of history to historiosophy.[46]

Hayek's philosophy is an effective rebuttal of this pretense. Man is always a participant in the social order. He cannot achieve an Archimedean point that confers apodictic certainty. Thus it is absurd to claim to remodel society according to intellectual plan. In Aristotle's terms, Cieszkowski's concept of *praxis* is really *poiesis,* or "making." The intellectual imagines himself in relation to society, not as a joint participant in a common order, but as a craftsman working with raw material to implement a design. This eschatological vision of the intellectual as demiurge characterizes all of the species of constructivism.

To a degree, Hayek's critique of constructivism can be expressed in the classical concepts of *sophia, theoria, praxis,* and *poiesis;* but this does not mean Hayek has returned to the classical position. He is dealing with a uniquely modern problem. Aristotle thought of *theoria, praxis,* and *poiesis* as three distinct ways of life. Politics was the sphere of *praxis.* It did not occur to him that intellectuals might redefine *praxis* as a combination of *theoria* and *poiesis* in an effort to "make" society according to plan. Yet this is precisely the situation that has made Hayek's critique of constructivism necessary.

It should be apparent that the constructivist redefinition of *praxis* as *poiesis* according to *sophia* destroys the specific character of politics. In Aristotle's classic exposition, politics is the field in which men encounter each other in action. Philosophy is concerned with the discovery and contemplation of unchanging truths, whereas practical wisdom *(phronesis)* is concerned with the changing data of human action and interaction. Precisely because apodictic knowledge is impossible, men must jointly work out the good life. It cannot be "made" because there is no plan or blueprint to serve as a guide. Politics cannot be an art *(techne)* like architecture, in which an idea is methodically given form. Political order can emerge only from a process of interaction; it cannot be designed from the *gnosis* of constructivist intellectuals. Hayek's critique of constructivism is a step toward the emergence of politics from ideological eclipse.

Notes

1. Cited in Fritz Machlup, ed., *Essays on Hayek* (New York: New York University Press, 1976), p. xv. Hayek shared the Nobel Prize with Gunnar Myrdal.
2. F.A. Hayek, *The Road to Serfdom* (Chicago: University of Chicago Press, 1944); *Law, Legislation and Liberty,* 3 vols. (Chicago: University of Chicago Press, 1973-79); *The Counter-Revolution of Science* (New York: Free Press, 1955); *Individualism and Economic Order* (Chicago: University of Chicago Press, 1948); *Studies in Philosophy, Politics and Economics* (Chicago: University of Chicago Press, 1967); *New Studies in Philosophy, Politics, Economics and the History of Ideas* (Chicago: University of Chicago Press, 1978). A bibliography of Hayek's works, complete through the early 1970s, will be found in Machlup, *Essays on Hayek,* pp. 51-59.
3. Arthur Seldon, ed., *Agenda for a Free Society* (London: Institute of Economic Affairs, 1961); Machlup, *Essays on Hayek.*
4. Gerald P. O'Driscoll, Jr., *Economics as a Coordination Problem* (Kansas City: Sheed, Andrews & McMeel, 1977); Norman P. Barry, *Hayek's Social and Economic Philosophy* (London: Macmillan, 1979).
5. Barry, *Hayek's Philosophy,* p. xi.
6. This section is an altered and expanded version of Thomas Flanagan, "F.A. Hayek on Property and Justice," in *Theories of Property: Aristotle to the Present,* ed. Anthony Parel and Thomas Flanagan (Waterloo, Ontario: Wilfrid Laurier University Press, 1979), pp. 336-40.
7. *Law, Legislation and Liberty,* vol. 1, chap. 2. Hereafter cited as *LLL.*
8. Adam Ferguson, *An Essay on the History of Civil Society* (London, 1767), p. 187, cited in ibid., p. 150.
9. Michael Polanyi, "The Republic of Science," *Minerva,* 1962, pp. 54-73.
10. F.A. Hayek, *The Confusion of Language in Political Thought,* Occasional Paper No. 20 (London: Institute for Economic Affairs, 1968).
11. *LLL,* 1:88-89.
12. Barry, *Hayek's Philosophy,* p. 88.
13. *LLL,* 1:38-39.
14. Bertrand de Jouvenel, "Order vs. Organization," in *On Freedom and Free Enterprise: Essays in Honor of Ludwig Von Mises,* ed. Mary Sennholz (Princeton, N.J.: Van Nostrand, 1956), pp. 41-51.
15. *LLL,* 1:154-55; Adam Smith, *Theory of the Moral Sentiments,* pt. 6, chap. 2; Karl Popper, *The Open Society and Its Enemies,* 4th ed. (New York: Harper, 1963), 1:202-3.
16. Bertrand de Jouvenel, *Sovereignty* (Chicago: University of Chicago Press, 1957), chap. 7.
17. *LLL,* 2:108.
18. Ibid., 2:134.

THOMAS E. FLANAGAN

19. F.A. Hayek, *The Use of Knowledge in Society,* Studies in Economics No. 3 (Menlo Park, Calif.: Institute for Humane Studies, 1977), p. 8; revised reprint of article from *American Economic Review* 35 (1945).
20. Hayek, *The Constitution of Liberty,* p. 59.
21. Ibid., chap. 4.
22. F.A. Hayek, "Kinds of Rationalism," in *Studies in Philosophy, Politics, and Economics,* pp. 82-95.
23. F.A. Hayek, "The Errors of Constructivism," in *New Studies in Philosophy, Politics, Economics and the History of Ideas,* pp. 3-22.
24. Ibid., p. 3.
25. *LLL,* 1:14.
26. Hayek, "Errors of Constructivism," pp. 8-9.
27. Ibid., p. 5.
28. *LLL,* 2:17-24.
29. Ibid., 2:44-61.
30. For Hayek's view of Comte, see *The Counter-Revolution of Science,* pp. 168-88.
31. F.A. Hayek, "The Repercussions of Rent Controls," in *Rent Control: A Popular Paradox,* ed. M.A. Walker (Vancouver, B.C.: Fraser Institute, 1975), pp. 67-83.
32. *Nicomachean Ethics* V. 2-3. Here Aristotle explains distributive justice with respect to the constitution, which is an organizational problem.
33. *LLL,* 2:62-100.
34. Barry, *Hayek's Philosophy,* p. 184.
35. *L'Esprit des lois* V. 13.
36. Stuart R. Schram, *The Political Thought of Mao Tse-tung* (New York: Praeger, 1963), p. 253.
37. Eric Voegelin, *Science, Politics and Gnosticism* (Chicago: Henry Regnery, 1968).
38. *Apology,* pp. 21-23.
39. G.W.F. Hegel, *Phänomenologie des Geistes,* Vorrede, 5.
40. *Metaphysics* I. 2.
41. Nicholas Lobkowicz, *Theory and Practice* (Notre Dame: University of Notre Dame Press, 1967), p. 8.
42. Eric Voegelin, *Order and History* (Baton Rouge: Louisiana State University Press, 1957), 3:268.
43. Hayek, *The Constitution of Liberty,* p. 64.
44. Lobkowicz, *Theory and Practice,* p. 205.
45. André Liebich, ed., *Selected Writings of August Cieszkowski* (London: Cambridge University Press, 1979), p. 55.
46. Ibid., p. 60.

Commentary
The Residue of Constructivism
TILO SCHABERT

Who would deny that we live in an age of spiritual confusion, in a world of false beliefs, in a fool's paradise surrounded by the shatters of vain attempts to subject the cosmos of life to the whims of man? The magic of secular prophecies promising man's perfection in this world is broken. Adherents still abound, but their creeds are reflections of power rather than testimonies of persuasion. The myth of infinite progress, meant to inject a historical meaning into man's conquest of nature, is found to be an empty conceit.

In the industrialized societies the Baconian pursuit of technological innovations continues, but from a different motive: There are necessities of economic survival and no longer any dreams of an immaculate "second nature," that is invented and graced by man. The idea of man as planner, creator, and master of his own world is dead—a matter of archeological interest if seen from the perspective of our para-modern experiences: the constraint of scarcity, the burden of uncertainty, the rediscovery of boundaries.

The critique of constructivism, then, cannot but attract our attention. It rebuts the delusive belief in man's unbounded power to plan his own fate; it argues against a confusion of classes in the general perception of human figurations and manifestations; it touches on the problem of meaning in man's history—the expectations of a quest for fresh sources of wisdom and counsel are elicited. Yet the diagnosis is given as therapy; the crucial questions are not posed; the predicament in which we find ourselves, living in this transitory age, is not at all alleviated.

TILO SCHABERT

"Order" and "Organization"

In the aftermath of the Enlightenment the importance of spontaneity in the conduct and the figurations of human life became eclipsed by a culture of rationalism. A greater emphasis on spontaneity would indeed provide a most appropriate remedy for the fury of "constructivist" policies. This choice of remedy, however, is hardly the problem—whereas the real difficulty would arise if an attempt were made to precisely identify instances of spontaneity in all the manifestations of human life. A distinction between "order" and "organization" is proposed that might be useful as a starting point. But it is much too general for being an adequate instrument of analysis. Esperanto might perhaps be correctly described as an artifact that falls into the class of "organization." Yet it is hard to believe that such languages as English, Italian, French, or German have "evolved spontaneously." Are we asked to suppose that Chaucer, Dante, Malherbe, or Luther never lived and never authoritatively shaped their respective languages?

The notion of "organization" probably corresponds with the common view of a business firm. But is the essence of a church correctly understood if it is similarly defined? Is the *corpus mysticum* just another "organization"?

Parallel questions could be asked with respect to all other illustrations presented in support of the proposed distinction. We are exhorted to rediscover the moments and possibilities of spontaneity in the conduct of our lives, and by way of incitement we are offered a display of improbable examples.

"Constructivism"

The slow disappearance of discredited ideas is always amazing. In the last third of this century the evidence of failures in all sorts of "planning"— social planning, urban planning, economic planning, governmental planning—is overwhelming. Nevertheless, if we look for them, we still find people addicted to the Comtean dream of a "scientific" solution to every problem. As critics of the contemporary world, we might be tempted to focus our attention on those people and their activities. In doing so, however, we would let ourselves be ensnared by the cold fascination of a lost cause. The problem of "constructivism" is no longer the problem posed by the ideologues of planning. The actual challenge is quite different: How could we still conceive of a truly human society after the modern deluge of totalitarian ideologies, reformist creeds, false prophecies? On which foundation could a community of human beings be built—or rather rebuilt—after this age in which man did everything to betray his humanity? Yes, we are all victims of this vain ambition to "construct" human society according to an abstract "plan"—to set up the perfect life on a *tabula rasa*. We know about all the despair, crimes, and death inflicted upon men by "constructivist" policies. Therefore—shall we ever be able again to entrust our fate to any man or any government? This—not the residue of "constructivism"—is the problem.

ATHANASIOS MOULAKIS

The Value of Work 5

One is struck, in considering work, by the extraordinary prestige
it enjoys. One wonders why a human activity that might reasonably be classed among the first in the order of necessity
should achieve such high rank in the order of value. This essay
attempts to reveal some misconceptions regarding the value of
work and to show that its glorification points to certain modes
of ideological transgression.

It is possible to distinguish in English between labor and
work. This distinction has been used by Hannah Arendt, in
whose hands it proved a heuristic device of great value. For
my purposes here I prefer to take the two terms together. To
John Locke, from whom Arendt borrowed the terms, the distinction between "the work of one's hands" and "the labour
of one's body" was in any case immaterial for his chief argu-
mentative concern of establishing a natural title to property.[1]

Work, as an exertion or effort directed to produce or ac-
complish something, is strictly instrumental and thus morally
indifferent. I am aware of a Hebraic usage of "work" that connotes, besides the sweat of one's forehead, the idea of service.
But such service is good or morally valuable insofar as it is in
the service of the living God in his justice. It is my contention
that it is an error to believe that work not only sets its goals
even as it pursues them but also sets the right goals simply by
being work, thus automatically ensuring its moral worth. It
is mistaken, I believe, to conceive work as an activity the very
exercise of which orients it toward the good, when it is perfectly
clear that one can indeed work toward evil ends. To try and
get out of the problem by saying, for instance, that loading stol-
en goods or laboriously faking banknotes is not "really" work

ATHANASIOS MOULAKIS

will not do, for it introduces an independent criterion of selection. The admission of independent criteria denies the autonomous worth of work. Again, the ingenious stratagem of calling work an act rather than an activity, common in the Hegelian tradition, is a willful blurring of useful distinctions that amounts to a confidence trick. I am also aware of the value attributed to work as *techne,* in which skill is stretched into conveying an experience of the structures of natural causality. But this admirable, indeed elating moment that is thought to bring together the act of making and the apprehension of (more or less) unchanging things leaves us in the dark regarding the rights and wrongs of actions of men living among their fellows in time. An ethical judgment on a particular piece of work is therefore dependent on the end that piece of work serves. There are axiological criteria, such as skill or workmanship, that apply independently of ends served, but they are not moral criteria. Work can be well done, beautifully executed, and so forth, and yet be base, salacious, or criminal. Thus, one speaks of a perfect crime. Admiration for, say, the perpetrators of the Great Train Robbery or the glorification of "romantic" crime figures ("Bonnie and Clyde") has no doubt diverse psychological causes, but one of them is precisely that the criminal act in its "freedom" transcends the humdrum and burdensome field of Work.

The fact that it suffices for some pieces of work to be formally admirable, for instance works of art, is a function of the formal, morally indifferent end in view of which they are executed or are seen by others to have attained. Even in a moderately developed economy, however, it is very difficult to know the ultimate use or end of a product or to predict the moral effects of a particular service. Allowance has to be made for fallible judgment and imperfect information, both of which are unavoidable in the contingency of historical existence in society. In the world of impersonal transactions "doing one's job" as "one works for the market" can be a passable rule of thumb. But it does not suppose or imply any moral value immanent in work itself.

In spite of all this, one's daily readings and one's everyday conversations suggest that "work" evokes positive connotations.

It would appear that all work, regardless of purpose, and only work is socially desirable, in the sense that it alone entitles one, for example, to emoluments or honors. All kinds of activities — including medicine, scholarship, art, government, and certainly commerce — try by way of justification to pass themselves off as work. The Prince of Wales, speaking recently to journalists, called his public activities his "job." The Chancellor of Bochum University has expressed pride in the fact that he ran the university like a *Betrieb* (a business or a factory), which I am happy to say is not quite true. If we are to believe Mr. Rossi-Landi, even speech is work; it is an extreme attitude, no doubt, that seeks to transform the agitator and bandier of words into a "worker." It is, moreover, an attitude that assumes that anything capable of becoming a marketable commodity, such as words, must have its origin in work. It is, of course, true that many activities can be conceived metaphorically as work. But over-burdening the metaphor leads to confusion, and it seems therefore preferable to restrict the meaning of work to the morally indifferent field, in Aristotle's terms, of producing external goods, whether these be destined for use or consumption, whether they be objects, facilities, or services. But it is, of course, just exactly because this field is not considered morally indifferent that activities not truly belonging to it seek to encroach upon it by means of extended metaphor. One might call these activities peacocks in crow's feathers.

Work is greatly valued as a *divertissement: "Travaillons sans raissoner, c'est le seul moyen de rendre la vie supportable."*[2] Voltaire's aperçu has at least the virtue of being straightforward. Max Weber's capitalist businessmen need a little more coaxing before they admit, even to themselves, the dreamy truth:

> If one asked them the "meaning" of the restless chase, which never leads to the enjoyment of one's own property, and which precisely given an innerworldly orientation must appear utterly meaningless, they would answer . . . "the concern for children and grandchildren"— more often however . . . and more accurately simply that Business with its constant work has become "indispensable to their life." This is in fact the only real motive which from the point of view of personal happiness manifests

the *irrationality* of a way of life in which a man exists for his Business and not the other way round.[3]

Work in this sense is not yet an instrument of rebellion against the human condition, a condition determined by man's mortality and his awareness of it, but it is a flight from the human condition into that fuss and bustle that Plato thought incompatible with justice. A statement of this incompatibility transposed into the aestheticist categories of Nietzsche's cultural criticism takes the form of the following tirade:

> Already one is ashamed of quiet rest; long reflexions cause pangs of conscience. One thinks watch in hand just as one lunches with an eye on the stock-exchange report. One lives as though one were constantly about to miss something. Rather do anything than nothing — this principle is another line along which to attack all culture *(Bildung)* and higher taste; and as all Forms are beaten to the ground by this hurry of people working, all feeling for Form itself is annihilated. One has no time and no energy for ceremonies any more, for roundabout manifestations of attachment, for the spirit of conversation, for any *otium* whatever. . . . The real virtue now is how to do something in less time than another. . . . Work has won over all good conscience to its side. The inclination to enjoyment calls itself a need for recreation and is ashamed of itself. "One owes it to one's health" one says when one is caught on a country outing.[4]

And Nietzsche will ask, not without advancing some adventurous answers of his own, *for whom* are all these people slaving away? The conception of a finality, and therefore of the moral worth of one's work as such, can be conveyed by an idea of great emotional power: working "for society." It is, as we saw, quite difficult to pursue concretely the connections of a particular contribution to a more general and vastly complex whole. But that is not all: Although all productive labor adds no doubt to the overall wealth of the society and contributes a part of the "fund" created by the "annual labour of a nation," it nevertheless requires a very considerable emotional leap to allow one to perceive all work, including, say, the making of "Saturday night specials"— and on what grounds could one exclude them from the "annual labour of the nation"?—as "working for," that is, as a "working for" the good of society.

It has been argued, of course, in a number of ways that the moral end of working for society can be realized independently of the motives—moral or otherwise—of the individual worker, or, maybe better, realized independently of the individual worker perceiving and being guided by such a universal end. A certain moment of automation of this sort is involved in Luther's conception of *Beruf,* or a calling, which makes through its effect the accomplishing of one's appointed task in Christian obedience—whatever its particular nature may be—a mode of active charity and of love for one's neighbor. But this providential effect of the division of labor is still informed by a quality that does not belong to simply working, namely, Christian obedience. The subjective motive retains its significance alongside the objective result. Furthermore, all callings and tasks executed in the spirit of Christian obedience are of value, not merely those that can be represented as modes of productive labor.

With the release from Christian obedience, the ethical result of working for the good of society appears paradoxically to be a function of work undertaken by each separate worker in order to fulfill elementary or self-seeking desires. It is, of course, the coordination of the diversity of pursuits that is supposed to work this miracle, the implication being that society is a closed system of economic exchanges, guided by an unseen hand, as a deistic optimism would have it, or by some more tangible manager. Whatever the strictly economic merits of the opposed views may be in this connection, the autonomous dignity of work seems achievable only at the price of closing society into a system and reducing man to a concupiscential accountant, not a rational but a calculating being.

But even allowing for ingenious mechanisms that transform private vices into public benefits—which is very different from the "Federalists' " prudent advice to form institutions in such a manner as to make every man's interest coincide as far as possible with the public interest—problems remain.

Working *for* something can be good only if that something is good. We can admit that working for society is good only if we know society or that particular society to be good. Otherwise, working for it would be ethically worthless or even reprehensible. The good citizen, said Aristotle, is relative to the regime; but the good man is not. From the knowledge that a democrat would be a good citizen of a democracy and a poor citizen of an aristocracy we cannot simply derive a judgment about his goodness as a man. This judgment would be dependent on a different set of considerations, unless we could show that one regime is in all significant ways—namely, the ways affecting man's humanity—demonstrably better than the other.

This argument is valid, unless the (mere) existence of society is equated with its meaning, or its essence is proclaimed to be identical with its existence and therefore is in some sense divine. This great being can then be faultless, despite the faults of its constituent parts: an immanent *realissimum*. Labor, the condition of mere existence, can be accordingly exalted as the essential human activity and play a significant part in diverse versions of this miraculous transfiguration.

And yet it is a matter of everyday experience that organized societies are perfectly capable of iniquities and crimes, and are always subject to imperfections. Although there is a lot of room for reasonable people to disagree, it is possible in principle to differentiate between one state of society and another.

To treat of work means to treat of practical philosophy to the extent that the shift in the importance of work as a topic of philosophical reflexion can be seen as a function or conversely as an indicator of changes of what practical philosophy is thought to be. For Aristotle, practical philosophy is not so much a philosophy *about* praxis, a body of abstract propositions about the field of action, as itself a *bios,* a manner of life qualified and informed by philosophy. Theory is not juxtaposed to action but is itself an elevated mode of action. The life of theory ranks, accordingly, higher than the other modes of the good life, that is, the political life and the life of pleasure. These three modes form a hierarchy but are not mutually exclusive. They complement each other in the fulfillment of the good life. The good life is action—*praxis*—and the end of action. As such it requires artifacts and, for that matter, the sustenance of mere life, but these are of value only insofar as they contribute to the good life. They are but means, albeit on occasion indispensable, necessary means. In this context, work is a subordinate activity; it is the production of outer goods ancillary to the practice of the good life, which is a movement of the realization of the *phusis* of man and of the optimal polis in the community of friends for the sake of the good.

Problems, such as the coordination of the three modes of life and the question of slavery, remain. But what is clear in Aristotle is that *primum vivere deinde philosophari* does not express an axiological order but one of necessary fact. It is necessary to live in order to philosophize; living does not, however, compel one to philosophize.

The potentially equal capacity of men to realize their *phusis* is faced with the empirical reality of the disparate actualization of the nature of concrete men. The problem, once perceived, can lead thinkers to posit, in their philanthropic pride, the realization of full humanity, the unencumbered epiphany of the human essence as *necessary*—like food and shelter are necessary—in *order* to show it to be the proper object of historical action or even the necessary end of history—a necessity as a sine qua non being speculatively assimilated to an *inevitability* in the course of events. We are faced with speculative attempts to revolutionize a necessary condition of the good life into its sufficient cause.

And yet, as Aristotle knew so well, it is precisely because of the impossibility of realizing a perfect polis in concrete historical existence that politics and political philosophy are needed.

Empires swept aside whatever meaning of life might be realized in the actual free citizenship of the polis. But they also showed up the largely accidental origin of people's station in life, servile or otherwise. Against such a historical background Stoicism modified the classical view of work. However, we find a Stoic understanding of work that goes beyond indifference toward occupations in an apolitical world. We find work as a positive instrument of virtue, as an exercise in self-control.

The Platonic and Aristotelian heuristic division of the soul hardens into a formal dualism of passionate body and rational mind. This reification is accompanied by a projection of reason as the law of the physical universe. Work as a methodical contact with the tissue of necessity, which has been proclaimed identical with divine reason, becomes an exercise in taming the passions. Reason has become for the Stoics a thing out there in the world. Aristotelian prudence *(phronesis),* the specific virtue of *praxis,* is, as we saw, itself *praxis;* the moral life is an unfolding of man's true nature in the erotic reaching toward the good, not in a compliance with a set of rules. Wisdom or the moral life consists no longer, according to the Stoics, in following Socrates but in "following nature," meaning the Natural Law "out there." It is man's special privilege or predicament to be able, unlike inanimate and instinctive beings, to choose not to follow nature. But he is well advised, in order to avoid the providential consequences of his folly, to exercise *(askein)* his virtue by complying to and obeying nature. And one of the principal modes of such obedience is work. Work, for the Stoics, finds a more than ancillary place in a conception of the moral life, which is not as with Aristotle a realization of one's nature and the fruition of one's human potentiality and thereby its own reward but is a compliance with a law "out there": an obedience. The practical fullness of the *bios* cedes to a theory *about* action.

The ascetic element certainly remains strong in the *labora* of St. Benedict's Rule. More significantly perhaps, the formula *ora et labora* unites the two poles of human experience. It balances man's condition of existence with his orientation toward a source of meaning. The value of labor is not autonomous. Nevertheless, the contact with the immanent ground of material existence as established by work corresponds formally to the meditative contact with the transcendent source of meaning in prayer, and is thus ennobled. Furthermore, the eschatological constitution of meaning is—like work—communicable with equal force, if not in an equal degree of differentiation to all, in a manner denied the *entelechy* of Aristotle's *bios.* It therefore is accessible to such as could not aspire to the freedom of the good polis. But the price of this equality or, historically, one of its conditions, is the disappearance of the polis.

The parallel between work and prayer is enhanced by both activities being subjected to rules: that is, being amenable to method. The historical importance of the rationalistically methodical qualities of Western monasticism—so different from the apophatic and anchoretic traditions of the Orthodox East—for the development of the Puritan temper and its secularization as "the spirit of capitalism," with a concomitant rise in the value attached to work, is too well known since Max Weber to need extensive comment.

Weber has pointed out the affinity between the monastic rules and the *regulae* of a Descartes. But the *ingenium* that the *regulae* seeks to regulate is taken to be creative in a manner alien to classical reason. It is a reason thought to be capable of *producing, generare,* in Hobbes' more explicit expression. Prudence is transformed into a practical knowledge of a different nature, into a *scientia propter potentiam.* It is obvious that work has a more crucial role to play in a practical philosophy thus transfigured. But we can only hope to pick such a *philosophie pratique,* Descartes reminds us, from the tree of general philosophy. It is the fruit of a luxuriant growth, the end of a philosophical enterprise that requires "the entire knowledge of all the Sciences."

The universality of the rationalist method holds out an egalitarian promise and by the same token ostensibly overcomes the difficulties raised by Aristotle's notion of philosophically informed praxis. The new method presents us, however, with problems of its own. The ancient notion did not presuppose the execution of a vast program leading to a *mathesis universalis,* nor did it require the philosopher to settle in a moral *provisorium* of conventionality until the accomplishment of the grandiose task.

But if the ingenuity of the Cartesian mind exalts the works of man, it applies itself to the task *"de faciliter tous les arts et diminuer le travail humain."* Work as labor, as *molestia,* remains a curse, which one may hope to diminish but which one has no reason to glorify.

It is Hegel who will take up the ascetic along with the productive aspects of work and place them in the service of *Bildung,* a conception of formation and education far more ambitious and far-reaching than the Puritan "formation of character." For Hegel, the self is not an original, autonomous starting point but is the result of a process, leading to the identification of the particular and the universal. The dialectical development of this secular equivalent of an *unio mystica* is what Hegel calls *Geist. Geist* is the coming together of particulars in the medium of a universal. The generality of such an universal is exemplified by what can be understood as belonging together when one speaks of "the spirit of the age." Mediums in which the particular merges with the universal are decisive elements in the enterprise of *Bildung.* In the early lectures held in Jena, Hegel sets out three such mediums or means *(Mitten):* language, work, and social interaction.

Work is a mean between man and nature, forming *(bildend)* both its object and its subject. It is not an instinctive or affective activity, but it has an intrinsic reasonableness insofar as work necessitates the suspension of the immediate satisfaction of desire and transfers the productive energies of the working subject to the object of work according to laws imposed on the self by nature. This contact of the spirit and man leads to the creation of instruments and the development of techniques. As Hegel argues: "The subjectivity of Work is raised to the level of a universal *(zu einem allgemeinen);* everyone can imitate it and work in the same manner; to that extent it is the permanent rule of Work."[5] The instruments, as it were, nail down the rule. Consciousness, estranged by its obedience to nature, is led back to itself by means of the technical rule, in the *sich zum Ding machen* of work. It emerges as "cunning consciousness" that "cheats" nature by turning it against itself. The machine embodies this cunning and mediates work utterly. This cheating does not, however, go unpunished. The interposition of machines does not obviate the necessity of work but simply transposes it so that it is no longer a juxtaposition of living spirit to living nature. Work itself becomes mechanical and degraded.

This is, of course, a *topos* that has been taken up by Marx in a grand manner. It is as remarkable as it is consistent with the attitude just adumbrated that Marx emphasizes the worth of work as an element of production rather than explore the diverse possibilities of distribution afforded by automation and high productivity. But questions of distribution seen independently of "anthropologically" interpreted modalities of production would have to be decided by criteria outside the work process itself. Such an attitude would not then permit the speculative rooting of the convergence of the particular and the universal — that is, the divinization of man — into a "system of needs" in which the necessary conditions eventually work out as sufficient causes. The admission of truly moral or even prudential criteria from outside the work process would undermine the assurance of achieving the *possessio salutis* in history. Already for Hegel, salvation, or whatever the symbolism for perfection and the good for man may be, is not something to be yearned for and approximated in the very yearning; it is a plateau to be reached, a thing to be possessed. In the Jena *Realphilosophie,* social interaction is, as we saw, alongside language and work a "means," in which love is characteristically realized, indeed *aufgehoben,* in the institution of marriage. And as Hegel proclaims, the purpose of his work is to move from mere love of knowledge to its actual possession.

The moral life requires objective ends in order to possess them. It is no longer, as with Aristotle, a tension, an eros, but the production of a status. This is why it is possible to mistake work for *praxis.* Work, in the words of Thomas Aquinas, can lead to a *perfectio facti,* not to a *perfectio faciendi,* unless, of course, the *faciendus* can be shown to be making himself. On the assumption that *vera sunt facta,* man's recognizing and in the same act realizing his true nature, requires that he produce it. Marx understood his master very well, even as he destroyed Hegel's philosophically multivalent and metaphysically overburdened work concept in favor of the "objectivity" or "thing-quality" of the economic category of labor.

And yet, if Marx seeks to revolutionize work into *praxis,* it is still in the desire to realize man's humanity as a *bios.* Thus, in the *Deutsche Ideologie* he focused on the *tätiger Lebenspro-zess,* the "active process of Life." He postulates a *Gesamtpraxis,* a total *praxis,* as the act of a being he calls the *Gesamtarbeiter,* the total worker. This *praxis* would take up the *aufheben* theory, a unification of theory and *praxis* to be achieved in the mode of *praxis.* Man grasping himself *(begreifen)* in a world of his creation has a precise formal parallel in classical theory: The highest possible activity of the highest possible subject is the unmoved mover contemplating himself. Only, the highest mode of *praxis,* the essential activity of man, Marx's supreme be-ing, is not contemplation but work, the production of things.

In the well-known second thesis to Feuerbach we read: "The question whether objective *(gegenständliche)* truth can be attributed to human thinking is not a question of theory, but is a practical quesiton."[6]

But the real practical question is whether objective, in the sense of reified, *gegenständliche* reality can be the measure of the truth of action. *Praxis* requires the use of products but can-not itself be produced.

Notes

1. My greatest debt is to the treatment of the question by Max Scheler, "Ethik und Arbeit," in *Frühe Schriften,* ed. Manfred Frings (Munich: Franke, 1970), pp. 161ff. Among the many other works from which I have profit-ed, I would like to mention particularly the discussion of practical phi-losophy in Arno Baruzzi, *Mensch und Maschine: Das Denken sub spe-cie Machinae* (Munich: Fink, 1973).

2. Quoted in Scheler, "Ethik und Arbeit," p. 190.

3. Max Weber, "Die Protestantische Ethik und der Geist des Kapitalismus," in *Gesammelte Aufsätze zur Religionssoziologie* (Tübingen: Mohr, 1972), p. 52.

4. Friedrich Nietzsche, "Die Fröhliche Wissenschaft," in *Werke,* vol. 5, book 2, ed. G. Colli and M. Montinari (Berlin: de Gruyter, 1973), pp. 236-37, par. 329.

5. G.W.F. Hegel, "System der Sittlichkeit," in *Schriften zur Politik und Rechts-philosophie,* ed. G. Lasson (Leipzig: Meiner, 1923), p. 428.

6. Karl Marx and Frederick Engels, *Selected Works in Three Volumes* (Mos-cow: Progress Publishing, 1965), 1:13.

Commentary
The Worthiness of Leisure
JOSIAH LEE AUSPITZ

In his unusually compact and suggestive essay Athanasios Moulakis makes two points and evokes a third. First, he argues
against the glorification of work as a good in itself. Second,
he uses the growing attention that philosophers have given to
the topic of work to sketch epochal shifts in the meaning of
practical philosophy and the relation of theory to practice. And
third, underlying his presentation of these two themes and en-
abling us to read it as sparkling and profound (rather than as
merely erudite and elliptical) is a considered, gentlemanly view
of politics and philosophy as requiring a leisured detachment
from the humdrum, workaday world.

Since it is the evocation of the third theme — the worthiness
of leisure — that gives the essay its considerable force, it would
seem niggling to focus too much attention on the specific arguments and examples employed. They should be read as a schol-
ar's poetry of reference rather than as a reference book in themselves. (It does not, after all, detract from Keats' poem that it
has Cortes instead of Balboa discovering the Pacific Ocean.)
Still, on two occasions Moulakis uses arguments that seem to
me to give away more than he intends.

To begin with, his case against the glorification of work
is structured on a rigid disjunction between means and ends.
Work he defines as "strictly instrumental and therefore morally indifferent." As pure instrumentality, it can have purely technical virtues, but these are never morally sufficient. To be of
moral worth, work must be employed toward a good end, a
criterion necessarily independent of the allegedly instrumental nature of work itself. This end, he shows, cannot be deduced
from some higher social good; the best such a deduction could

provide would be a doctrine of good citizenship, an arbitrary matter entirely relative to the given regime and (unless we are to accept an ameboid view of each regime as identical with a social organism) morally inadequate.

We can cheerfully assent to this line of argument until we try to proceed from its instrumentalist premises to an affirmative account of the ideal character of productive work. Then the conceptual apparatus on which it relies—the means-end disjunction—pulls us up short. Though widely accepted as a deliberative convenience, means-end reasoning has severe limitations in philosophy. Is it, indeed, ever philosophically adequate, even as a matter of stipulative definition, to posit a "strictly instrumental" means serving a variety of possible ends? Is the end ever adequately understood as a criterion exogenous to the means? Did Aristotle, who is often cited as the precursor of this way of thinking, really intend anything like our modern diremption of means from ends?

I think not, and more to the point, I think that Moulakis's deeper view depends on seeing why not. For he would have us understand work not as a self-satisfying but as a fragmentary aspect of life, drawing meaning, open-endedness, and moral force from its place in the larger context of a coherent way of life. On this view, the value of productive work lies not in its mere negation of idleness or sloth but in how it fits in with such other activities as leisured contemplation, virtuous deliberation, sensuous enjoyment, friendship, family support, philanthropy, or, as Moulakis eloquently encapsulates the Aristotelian summa of human aspiration, "the erotic reaching toward the good."

If some such higher striving is the "end" by which to judge work, it is so in the teleological sense of a principle of intelligibility and unfolding—a tension—rather than the utilitarian one of an end-state, end-product, or end-system of values—an equilibrium. As such, it cannot be fully independent of work but must be manifest in it. For if all human life is a reaching toward the good, work must show some evidence of this erotic striving or else be convicted of mere mechanism. Thus, while the notion of a "strictly instrumental" means may be adequate to the bare physical existence of tools (and even here I have my doubts), it cannot cover the human employment of tools that is commonly called work* and though there is a certain delicious irony in seeing instrumentalist categories used to dissolve one of the utilitarian superstitions of modern life, the rhetorical victory is Pyrrhic if it leaves untouched the stamp of these superstitions on our deeper categories of thought.

Wisely, Moulakis drops the means-end disjunction once it has served a forensic purpose and moves on to address the deeper shift in perspective of which both it and the glorification of work are a part. Here he proceeds with remarkable economy, using the topic of work in a few bold strokes to indicate three revolutions in the relation of theory and practice. The first is the emergence of what we now call the life of the mind, the *bios theoretikos,* theorizing as a practice, indeed, as the queen of practical activities. The second is the conception of

---

*As a logical matter, there are two ways to postpone the collapse of an instrumentalist definition, and Moulakis rejects both of them. The first is to define work as a morally indifferent *moment* of effort rather than the activity of which that effort is a part, as in the etymological relation between *ergon* and *energeia.* But this entails the distinction between act and activity that Moulakis rejects as a "confidence trick." (One might also see it as a trick borrowed from the infinitesimal calculus.) The second way out is to define work as the instrumental *mode* of human action, to be distinguished from, say, the moral mode, as in Croce's distinction between the economic and the ethical as "forms" of the practical. But if we are to posit an "instrumental mode" of human action it must be just that; it must take all human action as the substratum which it modifies and not merely activity aimed at the production of external goods and services. Again, this is a position that Moulakis rejects as stretching the concept of work too far. He stipulates instead *both* a modal definition of work as purely instrumental *and* a substantive limitation of it as covering production of all external goods and services. On the face of it, this mixed approach is less a definition than a disguised syllogism. It short-circuits all arguments and yields the conclusion that all production is "strictly instrumental and therefore morally indifferent"— a position that really cannot be associated with Aristotle's concept of *poesis,* which, as Moulakis later makes clear, refers not to a morally indifferent so much as a morally subordinate activity. In general, the distinction between making and doing should not be conflated with that between moral and instrumental modes.

a ramified body of public theorizing about practice, in which the point of the activity is not to live a life ennobled by leisured contemplation but to elucidate the moral law as part of a larger body of natural law. The third, announced in the New Philosophy of the seventeenth century, is to put a methodical kind of theorizing at the service of practice and to make utility in practice the test of such theorizing. Moulakis thus takes us on a tour from theory-as-practice to theory-about-practice to theory-for-practice. And since concepts derive their meaning from their relations, these shifting configurations of theory and practice are themselves evidence that different levels and genres of activity are being named with the selfsame Greek labels.

To limit each of these genres to its proper sphere, and to show how weaknesses in one may be complemented, opposed, or superseded by strengths in another, is, as I read it, the lasting contribution of Hegel's way of doing philosophy, and Moulakis is on the mark in assigning to Hegel a central place in his account. He presents Hegel as preparing the ground for the Marxian notion of man grasping himself in a world of his own creation through revolutionary *praxis*. The direct antecedents of the Marxian notion are, he shows, to be found both in Hegel's treatment of *Mitten* (mediums) and in his rhetoric about work and possession of knowledge in philosophy itself. And he is especially acute in observing that reliance on the work metaphor turns the moral life from an adventure, tension, or predicament into the production of a status.

For Moulakis's larger purposes, however, it is important to insist that all the talk about "possessing knowledge" and about the way in which work—particularly a philosophical work—offers an exhilirating medium of participation in the Absolute is not what the enduring Hegel is really about. In his mature treatise on logic Hegel limits the whole verbal metaphor of grasping and possession *(begreifen)* to the *Begriff,* a conceptual stage that is *aufgehoben* in the *Idee.* The philosophical criterion that Hegel then calls the *Absolute Idee* is thoroughly purged of the work metaphor. Hegel's *Absolute Idee* is not the possession of knowledge by union of the subject and object in language and work; on the contrary, it makes clear that such possession is always a mirage, that the important thing, as Hegel put it earlier, is the journey.

At the same time, Hegel does give full scope to work as the means by which to achieve objectively an end that is first subjectively conceived. Indeed, he understands the logical cogency of work when it is a means toward an end. It connects the end conceived with the end achieved and thus becomes the middle term in a syllogism *("Das Mittel is die Mitte des Schlusses." Science of Logic,* vol. 2, pt. 2, chap. 3, sec. B). But since neither syllogistic nor means-end reasoning (even in its correct teleological form) is for Hegel ultimately satisfactory, working and its products can provide only road markers, not destinations in themselves.

All this, of course, is exactly what Moulakis is saying, and so my two reservations about his presentation merely strengthen his main theme. The real counterpoint to work on his account is not *praxis* but the critical point of view from which we are able to discuss the relative satisfactions of both work and *praxis.* This point of view must be cultivated. Its prerequisite is a disciplined disengagement not only from production but from affairs in general—a leisured detachment that was once called *schole.* It is proof of the shifts that Moulakis sketches that *schole* itself was transformed first into the public disputation of scholasticism and then into "scholarship," increasingly defined as the publication of the fruits of scientific research—as work. As such, it is as far from the *bios theoretikos* as the Stakhanovite is from the citizen.

Notes on Contributors

JOSIAH LEE AUSPITZ is Director of the Project in Public Philosophy of the Sabre Foundation. His articles have appeared in *Political Theory, Public Interest, Commentary, American Spectator, Harpers,* and elsewhere.

FREDERICK M. BARNARD is Professor of Political Science at the University of Western Ontario. He has published *Zwischen Aufklärung und politischen Romantik* (1964) and *Herder's Social and Political Thought* (1965) and has edited *Herder on Social and Political Culture* (1969). His many articles have appeared in *Journal of the History of Ideas, Canadian Journal of Political Science, American Political Science Review, Journal of the History of Philosophy,* and elsewhere.

THOMAS E. FLANAGAN is Professor and Chairman of the Department of Political Science at the University of Calgary. He has published *Louis "David" Riel* (1979) and has edited *The Diaries of Louis Riel* (1976); with Glen Campbell and Gilles Martel, *Louis Riel: Poésies de Jeunesse* (1977); and with Anthony Parel, *Theories of Property: Aristotle to the Present* (1979). His articles have been published in the *Canadian Journal of Political Science, Canadian Psychiatric Association Journal, Canadian Ethnic Studies,* and elsewhere.

JURGEN GEBHARDT is Professor of Political Science at the Institute for Political Science at the University of Erlangen-Nürnberg. In addition to journal articles, he has published the following books: *Politik und Eschatlogie* (1963) and *Die Krise des Amerikanismus* (1976) and has edited *Die Revolution des Geistes* (1968) and *James Harrington* (1973).

VICTOR GOUREVITCH is Professor and Chairman of the Department of Philosophy at Wesleyan University. He has published articles in the *Journal of Philosophy, Review of Metaphysics, International Studies in Philosophy, History and Theory,* and elsewhere.

GEORGE J. GRAHAM, JR. is Professor of Political Science at Vanderbilt University. He has published *Methodological Foundations for Political Analysis* (1971), and *Post-Behavioral Era* (1972). With Scarlett G. Graham, he has edited *Founding Principles of American Government: Two Hundred Years of Democracy on Trial* (1977). He has published articles in such journals as the *Political Science Quarterly, Midwest Journal of Political Science,* and *Political Science Reviewer.*

WILLIAM C. HAVARD, JR. is Professor and Chairman of the Department of Political Science at Vanderbilt University. His many books include *Henry Sidgwick and Later Utilitarian Political Philosophy* (1959); *Government and Politics of the United States* (1965); and *Recovery of Political Theory: Limits and Possiblities* (1984). He has edited *The Changing Politics of the South* (1972); with David R. Mayhew, *Institutions and Practices of American Government* (1967); with Joseph L. Bernd, *200 Years of the Republic in Retrospect* (1976); and with Walter Sullivan, *A Band of Prophets: The Vanderbilt Agrarians After Fifty Years* (1982). His articles have appeared in the *Journal of Politics, Public Administration Review, Western Political Quarterly, Louisiana Law Review, Annals of the American Academy of Political and Social Science, Polity, Southern Review, Archiv für Rechts und Sozialphilosophie,* and elsewhere.

ATHANASIOS MOULAKIS is Professor of Political Science at the European University Institute in Florence, Italy. In addition to several articles, he has published *Homonoia: Eintracht und die Entwicklung einer politischen Bewusstsein* (1973) and *Die Politik der Askese: Simone Weil* (1980).

J. M. PORTER is Professor of Political Science at the University of Saskatchewan. He has edited *Martin Luther: Selected Political Writings* (1974) and has published articles in *Marxist Perspective, The American Journal of Jurisprudence, Denver Quarterly, The Journal of the History of Ideas,* and elsewhere.

TILO SCHABERT is Professor of Political Science at the University of Bochum. In addition to several articles, he has published *Natur und Revolution* (1969) and *Gewalt und Humanität* (1978), and he has edited *Der Mensch als Schöpfer der Welt* (1971) and *Aufbruch zur Moderne* (1974)

KLAUS VONDUNG is Professor of German Literature and Dean of the Department of Languages and Literature at the University of Siegen. He has published *Magie und Manipulation* (1971), *Volkischnationale und nationalsozialistische Literaturtheorie* (1973); and he has edited *Das wilhelminische Bildungsburgertum* (1976) and *Kriegserlebnis: Der Erste Weltkrieg in der literarischen Gestaltung und symbolischen Deutung der Nationen* (1970).